Planning the Pre-5 Setting

Practical Ideas and Activities for the Nursery

Christine Macintyre and Kim McVitty

David Fulton Publishers

Other titles of interest:

Exploring Early Years Education and Care Linda Miller, Rose Drury and Robin Campbell
Learning and Teaching in the Foundation Stage Pat Hughes
Enhancing Learning through Play Christine Macintyre
Planning an Appropriate Curriculum for Under Fives (Second edition) Rosemary Rodger

David Fulton Publishers Ltd
The Chiswick Centre, 414 Chiswick High Road, London W4 5TF

www.fultonpublishers.co.uk

David Fulton Publishers is a division of Granada Learning Limited, part of the Granada Media group.

First published 2003
10 9 8 7 6 5 4 3 2 1

British Library Cataloguing in Publication Data
A catalogue record for this book is available from the British Library.

ISBN 1 84312 058 5

Typeset by FiSH Books, London
Printed and bound in Great Britain by Ashford Colour Press Limited, Gosport, Hants

Contents

Acknowledgements

There are many people who have worked hard to make this book possible and our thanks go to them all. Special mention must be given to the nursery staff – Mrs Deborah Wilson, who read and commented on the text, Miss Louise Baigrie and Miss Debbie McKenzie, other practitioners who contributed ideas, reflections and many pertinent observations. As they teach, their enjoyment of the children and their achievements shines through. We hope we have managed to capture at least some of that spirit in the text.

A huge thank you also to all the children who inspired us to carry on writing because they were so anxious to see their photographs in a real book! We thank their parents for giving permission for these photographs to be published. We hope that everyone enjoys seeing the children learning, discovering and problem solving in a colourful, friendly setting. If they do, our efforts will have been worthwhile.

Introduction

This book aims to provide a clear and comprehensive guide to setting up a successful and happy nursery environment in either the private or the school sector. All the suggested planning and organisation were tried out, evaluated and retried until the staff were able to agree that a sensible and realistic 'way that works' had been found.

One of the considerations in writing the book is the knowledge that every nursery is different: the children, their parents, the staff and the setting itself all contribute to making the learning environment 'their own'. While no one would wish otherwise, this does mean that some of the ideas suggested may need some adaptation to suit another context. Some parents, for example, may wish to have more information in their nursery booklet, while others – perhaps those who find reading English difficult – may prefer to have less. This book offers guidance, not prescription. Nursery staff are experts at being resourceful and imaginative, so we hope that the structure and strategies suggested here will provide enough material to enable them to plan and organise their own setting in a way that leaves maximum time for supporting their own children.

A second point is that the curriculum documents for different regions vary in the ways in which they group the competences they wish the children to acquire. While the headings within the developmental frameworks are therefore different, e.g. in England mathematics has a column of its own while in Scotland it is included under the heading, 'Knowledge and understanding of the world', the key learning outcomes aimed at guiding the teaching are essentially the same. This is discussed in the text.

Just as the children learn new things every day, so do the staff. Observing and interacting with three- and four-year-olds in a way which enables them to thrive are very difficult skills that are not easily acquired. Yet the rewards – building relationships with the parents and carers who are partners in their children's education and seeing the children become happy, stimulated and increasingly independent learners – are such that most staff regard the nursery as the very best place to be!

1 Settling in

Attending a playgroup or nursery for the first time is an important milestone in the lives of many children and their parents. It may be the first time parents have entrusted their children to 'strangers' and the first time that these children have had to cope without their parents at their side. Some will anticipate the new venture confidently while others will need more reassurance that good things lie ahead. So that everyone can relax and enjoy this new stage in the children's lives, it is vitally important that right from the start, a relationship of trust between parents and nursery staff is established. This chapter shows how that may be done.

What do the children need to know?

While many children come into nursery ready to hang their coat on their peg and 'have a go', others need lots of reassurance to help them settle in. This may be the first time they have experienced:

- being 'left' with people they do not know;
- being among so many children, all busily employed;
- having so much space and so many toys;
- not being sure that Mum will come back.

They need to know that they are welcome to join in, that they can settle at their own pace with Mum beside them, that they can choose what they want to do and that they will soon make friends.

To prevent the children, especially the three-year-olds, becoming overwhelmed by all that goes on in the nursery, it is a good idea to make the first visit a short one of an hour or so. It is best if the child goes home before story time as sitting closely within a group could prove too much for the first day. Even although Mum is there in the background, it is better for the children to leave after a short, happy spell – then they will be anxious to come back tomorrow! Visits can gradually be lengthened, with mums absent for increasingly longer spells once the children have understood the layout of the nursery, the routine of the day and when they have recognised that they will be safe and supported in this new environment.

What do parents need to know?

Parents who do not know the nursery or the staff are likely to require plenty of reassurance too. They need to know that:

- the nursery is a safe place for their children;
- their children will be valued as individuals and well cared for;
- the staff are qualified to teach very young children;
- their children will be supported and encouraged to learn;
- if any difficulty arises (e.g. the child not settling in or feeling ill), they will be contacted immediately.

Kiera and Hannah are supported as they learn

Practical details

Parents need to be sure of:

- the start and end times of their child's session;
- the number to call if they have a problem, e.g. their child is unwell or they are going to be late collecting their child;
- how to advise the nursery staff if any other person has their permission to collect their child – this is essential for security.

What does the nursery need to know?

Parents need to provide essential information before any child can be left at the nursery.

Personal details

The nursery will need to have:

The child's name and date of birth.

Parents' names, home addresses and telephone numbers.

Any workplace telephone numbers (for emergencies only).

Details of a second reliable contact (name, telephone number, distance from the nursery).

Details of anyone else authorised to collect the child from nursery.

The name and telephone number of the child's doctor and/or health visitor.

Any dietary information, e.g. food that must not be offered at snack time.

Details of any allergies, e.g. asthma triggers such as dust or animal fur, or eczema that might be aggravated by the use of soap.

Information about previous or ongoing contact with a hospital, a speech and language therapist, a psychologist or social work agencies.

Details of the first symptoms of any recurring illness, particularly if a GP has to be contacted quickly (e.g. asthma, diabetes).

Details of any medication. If this has to be given during nursery, written instructions of the dose and how and when to administer it are required.

(Note: a medical form provided by the school has to be completed. This gives staff the authority to follow the instructions that have been given.)

If special resources are required, e.g. a handrail in the toilets and in the garden, the more notice the school has the better (see also Ch. 7, 'Transitions', p. 105).

Planning a first meeting between staff, parents and children

Although there is a great deal of administration to get through at a first meeting, some quality time must be scheduled for parents to ask questions and for the staff to share their plans and hopes for the coming session. The date of the first meeting needs to be carefully planned to give staff time to talk – ideally once the nursery is up and running and when the returning children have re-established their routines and their relationships with the staff.

It is a good idea to make special arrangements for parents coming into the nursery with their children for the first visit, depending on whether a home visit has already taken place (perhaps at the end of the previous term). All parents are offered such a visit but some families, for a number of reasons, may not have been able to participate and so some 'new starts' will be unknown.

Home visits

Two staff together arrange to visit the children's homes, leaving precise details of the times and places of their visits (and their mobile phone numbers) with the remaining nursery staff. This preliminary meeting ensures that staff and parents are acquainted with each other before the first day at nursery. It allows the staff to see the children interacting with their parents, to understand a little of the home background and to begin to consider how much and what kind of support that particular child will require during the first days at nursery.

From these meetings the staff can decide the order of the children coming for their first visit. If they anticipate that one particular child will need special support, that child can come in as a 'single' whereas another two children with their parents could attend the same session – one at 9.30am and another at 10.00am.

It is important for all parents to feel that the staff have had the opportunity to talk with them individually and establish the first all-important, friendly link. This time allows the parents to see the nursery in action and gives the staff advance notice of strategies which might help their child settle down. If, for example, a particular child is keen on cars, the staff can set out some toy cars for his first visit to the nursery. A 'staggered start' or 'gradual entry' also prevents the nursery being swamped by adults! Organisational considerations such as these will help the staff to understand each child and provide the most appropriate support.

At a first meeting, there is no need to bombard parents with too many questions, for as the relationship between the nursery and the family develops, understandings will be built up which will make sharing information easier. From the start however, parents should be made aware of the importance of sharing details of everyday happenings in their child's life. Even small snippets of information, e.g. that the goldfish has just died, can explain why the child is upset and enable the staff to give the most appropriate kind of comfort or if a child has refused breakfast, staff can ensure that an early snack is made available. In the latter case, staff could then check whether the child was willing/able to eat and if they find a problem this can be related back to the parents. The parents have to appreciate why this kind of personal information is needed or they could resent giving it!

Sharing personal information

Useful information which could be passed on at this first meeting (or subsequently shared at arriving and leaving times) might concern any parental worries. Parents might have suspicions that 'something' is wrong with their child; perhaps, in their eyes, he or she is not progressing as fast as a sibling or other children of the same age and they would like the staff to confirm/deny this or initiate requests for specialist support. Maybe another child is showing signs of temporary difficulties due to changing circumstances or the arrival of a baby in the family, and the staff need to understand why the child's behaviour is affected.

Understandably, some parents may find it difficult to share personal information or concerns about their child, suspecting perhaps that they might be considered bad or inadequate parents. In these instances, do not rush them but allow a little more time to discuss what both parties can do to help the children settle in – perhaps over a cup of tea. This will smooth the path of future communications!

Parents might also wish to explain:

- that their child needs to be reminded to go to the toilet;
- that their child's speech is slow or that they have difficulty making themselves understood;
- that they suspect their child has a hearing difficulty;
- that they have recently moved to the area, the child is missing his or her old home and has not yet had the opportunity to make friends with the local children.

Getting to know the child's world

At nursery, children are encouraged to talk to the staff; they expect the staff to know their cat's name, that Auntie Sharon lives next door and that they have a big brother – often in that order of importance. Conversations can break down if the staff have insufficient background information to reply appropriately.

Helpful insights might concern:

- the number of other children in the family and their names;
- whether the child attending the nursery is the oldest or youngest;
- which schools any siblings attend;
- whether one or both parents are at home when the child is at nursery;
- whether one or both parents speak English fluently;
- what religion the family observes;
- whether the child has had any previous nursery experience;
- the names of people in daily contact with the children;
- any pets and their names.

Staff who do not live close to the nursery could also carry out some research. Their first conversations will be more relevant if they know something of the local area and the people who live there. While no one should make any assumptions, understanding the children's homes, their family arrangements and possibly what amenities are available to them, e.g. local shops, a library or a garden, can help interactions to be correctly pitched and will avoid the possibility of causing hurt or embarrassment to anyone.

As can be seen from the above, a great deal of forward planning is needed to ensure that the children, their parents and the staff get off to a good start. This comes through understanding and trusting each other's position and working together to achieve the same goals.

Confidentiality

The first meeting is a time for trust and partnership to be established. Although staff must collect personal information, the parents must be reassured that this will be held in the strictest confidence and that no information will be passed on to any outside agency without their permission.

Permission slips

[Name and address of nursery
Date]

Dear Parent/Carer,

During the nursery session, opportunities arise for the children to go on outings such as visits to the local shops, to the farm or the zoo. Notice of outings beyond the local environment will always be given, but a cover note giving us permission to take your child out of school would be helpful. It goes without saying that the children will be properly supervised.

Please sign here if you give permission for outings:

Signature.. Date.....................

There is also the possibility that requests will be made for photographs or filming the children as they enjoy their activities. These may be used in teacher training or in text-books for teachers.

Please sign here if you agree to photos and/or films:

Signature.. Date.....................

If you do not wish your child to participate, please return the tear-off slip by [date].

- -

I do not wish...... [Child's name].........to go on outings.

I do not wish ......[Child's name].........to be photographed or filmed.

Signature.. Date.....................

Thank you for completing this form.

A.N. Other (Head Teacher)

Figure 1.1 Permission slip

At an early meeting, it is useful to ask parents to sign a permission slip which covers 'films, photos and local outings'. This prevents the need for repeated requests, but parents should also be made aware that they can cancel their permission if circumstances change. Similarly, if the nursery is expecting a visit from 'outsiders' (perhaps for a 'People who help us' session), parents need to know that they have been approved by the school.

Inform parents that details of any 'event' will be posted on the parents' notice board well in advance so that they can react to it as appropriate.

Preparing a 'Welcome' booklet for parents

Different parents will need different amounts of information. Some nurseries provide lists of their aims for a session and give detailed plans of how these are to be achieved, but some parents will find a smaller booklet more manageable and appropriate. It is up to the staff to gauge what is most suitable for their particular parents. A smaller booklet can be extended by daily bulletins on the parents' notice board.

First impressions are very important. Ideally, the front cover of the booklet should include the word 'Welcome' in several languages (including, of course, all the first languages of the children in the nursery).

Figure 1.2 Suggested front cover of booklet with 'Welcome' written in different languages

Even if the children all speak English, they learn implicitly that children from every culture are welcome and that different languages use different symbols to record their speech. A booklet with user-friendly language and illustrated by line drawings to convey a sense of fun will help parents who have little or no English to understand something of the nursery day; it will also be of help to first-language English-speaking parents who have reading difficulties.

Such a booklet has several other benefits. If it is handed out at the start of the meeting, it will:

- allow parents to relax, safe in the knowledge that they can recap information from the booklet later;
- let parents study the information at their own pace and discuss what it means in practical terms for their own child – perhaps they need to check emergency numbers, work out the time it will take buses from their place of work to reach the nursery, or arrange rotas with other parents;
- provide a list of staff names and nursery contact numbers thereby giving parents a reference document they can use throughout the year;
- act as a reminder, e.g. that children should not come in their best clothes as the activities can be messy (such as painting and gluing);
- provide a first line of communication if parents were unable to attend the first meeting and sent a substitute instead;
- let parents know how they can become helpers in the nursery.

Parents with little or no English

Staff have to plan to ensure that time is made available to convey accurate information to parents whose first language is not English. This is especially important at the start of nursery because a means of contacting the parents will have to be established. Perhaps just getting over the message that a phone call that says 'Nursery' means that they have to collect their child immediately would be the best start, for then they know that they will be contacted should their child be unhappy or unwell.

Thereafter, establishing daily contact is important. Even just one minute when the child arrives one day and five minutes the next day when the child is collected is enough to establish trust. Apart from the language difficulties, these parents may not be at all familiar with this kind of preschool education. At home they may not have shared the same stories with their children or played the same games, and they may be very anxious as to how they will get on with the other children who have the same kind of family life and traditions to talk about.

Hopefully the stage will be reached when the parents will feel comfortable joining their child in the nursery for a short time and then sharing some aspects of their culture with all the other children, perhaps by contributing to a festival input. This authenticity would extend the education of the other children – and maybe the staff too.

Interpreters

In many regions it is possible to arrange help from interpreters, but usually they have to be booked in advance and so are not available for any unexpected or urgent communication. In these instances there are a number of strategies that could be employed:

1. Other parents in the school may be prepared to act as 'buddys' or interpreters. They may know of someone who lives close to the parents who would be prepared to help or they may know where they could shop for specific items. If the parents are happy with this suggestion, it could ease settling in.
2. Similarly, another child from an older class could come into the nursery for a while to help the new child settle. This would depend on the nursery child's needs: some children can feel swamped by being looked after or resent being made to look different from the other children. Some children could even acquire 'learned helplessness', i.e. letting others do what they could quite easily do for themselves! This could be a barrier to the children becoming independent and making their own decisions.

3. Perhaps the nursery could send a dual language book home for the parent and child to read together first. Then the story can be read in English at story time in the nursery. The English as an additional language (EAL) child, already familiar with the story, can then relate to the happenings within it as it is being read and so feel part of the group.

Inviting parents to help

Staff will gradually come to know the parents and how to encourage them to help in any way they might feel comfortable. Some parents will have particular talents to share, e.g. making dressing-up clothes or playing the piano for singing games; others may prefer to start in a 'resources manager role', e.g. helping to prepare resources in the nursery such as gathering pine cones for the nature table or collecting junk for gluing at home, thus keeping the supply topped up. This kind of activity is more manageable for parents who have a baby at home; they can come into the nursery to read stories or help with baking once they have more free time. Others will enjoy helping with fund raising or baking cakes for parents' meetings. Some parents will want to help but may doubt that they have anything worthwhile to offer.

How can they be encouraged?

One suggestion is to list 'helping possibilities' on the parents' notice board and ask parents to choose one. This will help them to realise that no contribution is too small – the complex organisation of a nursery has room for many kinds of contributors. Parents should be made aware that time rather than money is what is required. Some parents may be able to obtain off-cuts of wood (for woodwork) or linoleum (a small blue piece can be shaped to make a pond for small world activities) which would only be discarded from their workplace; others may be able to supply computer paper that has been used on one side but could provide space for painting on the other. Yet again others may be able to supply cardboard cartons of different shapes and sizes! Many items of junk are highly prized in the nursery. Through collecting or helping – even in a small way – parents with no previous experience can begin to understand and participate in their children's education.

After the first attempt, some parents may still retain doubts about their contribution and will need reassurance and encouragement to give them the confidence to continue. Praising even small successes is the way forward, e.g. 'The way you encouraged Jane to share the glue tub with Peter was just great. She usually finds that difficult and will just walk away rather than share. Well done!'

Of course there are other parents who will require help to interact with the children in a child-centred way, i.e. respecting the children's ideas and preferences, and not turning their own good idea into a project in which they do all the planning and the children are just there to watch or fetch and carry! This can be difficult to explain without offending the parents who may have taken some time to think their idea through.

Many visitors to the nursery exclaim at the confidence and skill shown by even three-year-olds. How have they developed this assurance? While everyone acknowledges the part played by the home and the community, i.e. the early environment, the opportunity to cope as an independent being may not present itself until the children can stay at nursery on their own and enjoy all that is on offer there. The next chapter is devoted to an explanation of the ethos of child-centred education and how in nursery, all aspects of the children's development are nurtured. This provides children with the confidence and competence to make the most of their time in a happy, positive environment.

2 Explaining the child-centred ethos of the nursery

Child–centred learning is based on the observation of the children by the staff, recognition of both their interests and their readiness to learn, i.e. their developmental stage, and the provision of activities and teaching support which will encourage them to learn more. This is a good way to learn because the children themselves choose what they want to do and so they are motivated to persevere. The level of challenge is also likely to be appropriate. The staff observe the children closely so that they can record the activities they have chosen and how well they do them. They also note those the children avoid and the skills and abilities which need support if a wider range of activities is to be tackled and enjoyed. All of this information helps staff to build a picture of each 'whole' child.

Helping parents to understand child-centred education

At the early stages, staff should attempt to discover – very subtly – how much the parents know about nursery education so that they can appreciate how much explanation different parents wish to/should have. Parents who have had other children in a nursery are usually delighted to offer support but otherwise are happy to 'let the staff get on with it', confident that they are doing the right thing. Most new parents will be anxious to learn; once their child has settled they are likely to marvel at the amount of careful planning, organising and teaching that goes on. But a few will have fixed – and often unrealistic – ideas about what their children 'should do' in nursery. If, for example, they want their children to learn to read and write from Day 1, then they need explanations of the preliminary stages and how these are built up in a child–centred way according to each child's stage of development.

Some parents may not know what to expect at all and will need time to observe their children taking part in the various activities. Staff should explain and/or demonstrate how the children's learning is enhanced through play by pointing out the potential for learning in each area (see Ch. 3, p. 27), and by asking parents to appreciate the experienced children's confidence and competence.

Just playing?

Parents new to the nursery environment may well think that the children are 'just playing', but to these very young children, play and learning are synonymous. Many authors have tried to describe play and have even claimed that 'trying to describe play is like trying to catch the wind in a paper bag' – a lovely picture but not very helpful for people trying to understand! However, there are criteria which attempt to describe play and these at least show why it is so popular.

Criteria for play

For an activity to be called 'play', it should:

- be enjoyable, freely chosen by the children;
- be an activity done for its own sake, i.e. without any need;
- be able to produce an end product;
- be voluntary – the children should be able to choose what they wish to do and stay with that activity or abandon it at will;
- bear some relationship to something that is not classed as play.

The last criterion is quite strange, but reflecting on nursery activities helps to clarify the issue. Think of children in the house corner. They are practising lots of activities they have seen their parents do such as tidying up, setting the table, dusting, making the bed – all of these are real-life activities carried out in miniature, and possibly willingly because the children have made the decisions for themselves! Important too is the fact that the children know that the house belongs to them and that adults will only enter if invited to do so.

Generally, free flow play is the order of the day. Children choose how they are going to spend their time. Staff offer activities but the children decide whether to attend, what to do and how long to continue each particular one.

At the start of the nursery year, children are allowed a great deal of free play which they can choose and abandon at will. But once they have settled down and had the opportunity to try things out, staff will encourage them to stay to complete a piece of work and to try activities that they might, left to their own devices, tend to avoid. Praise is the most successful strategy combined with support when it is requested. Children usually love to have something – a painting or a gluing – to take home. Unfortunately, one of the lessons children have to learn is that some things they have made cannot be taken away with them at the end of the day! Perhaps a construction or a robot has to stay in the nursery and eventually be dismantled. This can be hard for children to accept, but if parents come in to admire the piece as part of a display, then the children usually come to understand and accept the 'rule'.

Some researchers (Bee 2000; Macintyre 2001a, 2002) have studied play within a developmental framework, i.e. an ages and stages approach. They have subdivided play into the different kinds which appear as the children mature (see Table 2.1).

As children change in stature and capability, so too does the type of play in which they engage. As they develop new motor skills, they can handle objects with greater dexterity and so they 'outgrow' the sensory motor play which provides important information about the properties of objects and become involved in construction play. And as children fit different objects together or build one on top of another, they are probably working at the midline of the body and learning about hand dominance, an important developmental skill which helps writing and all the fine motor skill activities which are needed. The nursery curriculum is full of practical activities which depend on these basic competences; coping at home requires them too.

As children grow, they also become less egocentric, i.e. increasingly able to see the world from another person's perspective, and this is the basis for pretend play. This occurs in two stages. The first, i.e. 'symbolic play', is when the children use an object to represent something else (e.g. a yo-yo becomes a dog on a lead). The second stage, i.e. 'pretend play', is when the children actually take on the role of another person and enact that person's duties. The final play stage (around the age of seven) is when children are able to follow the rules of a game. While these stages are not fixed as such – and teachers will always recognise children who are well ahead, those who are slower to develop and those whose insecurity leads to temporary regressions to an earlier stage – they do provide a way of monitoring progress.

Table 2.1 Play: a changing experience

Type of play	Age	Characteristics
Sensory/motor: early discovery about shape/ texture/weight/taste/ hardness/if shape can change	0–2 solitary play	Exploration and perception: child seeing/feeling/listening to learn about objects
Symbolic play: first signs of imagination/pretending	2–4 parallel play, i.e. playing near another child without cooperating and interacting	Using one object to represent another (a yo-yo is a dog). Having an imaginary friend
Simple construction: early recognition of simple > complex		Building towers – Lego, roads in the sand etc.
Pretend play: imaginative/fantasy play. Role play in context	4+ with a friend	Taking on the characteristics of someone else in their setting, e.g. nurses in a hospital or workers on a construction site
Games with rules: Scrabble, chess, dominoes, football. Can create rules for a made-up game	7+ in a same sex group	Following rules and checking others do. Bending the rules to win!

Some children will not follow the more usual developmental pattern – perhaps they can play a mean game of chess without being able to pretend at all. While this is less usual, observing play preferences like this can indicate that teachers need to discover whether the lack of pretending is a strong preference for logic and reality or a sign that a specific learning difficulty is looming. This would need to be carefully monitored. Observing children at play, i.e. in a stress-free environment, enables assessments like this to be made.

It is fascinating to realise that no one tells the children when to move on from one play stage to the next: they are perfectly capable of deciding for themselves. In times of stress, however, they may revert to an earlier kind of play or repeat the same action over and over again. These signs can tell the nursery staff that something is amiss. So play has a therapeutic as well as a diagnostic function.

Fostering learning in all aspects of development

Nursery staff aim to foster the children's learning in all aspects of their development because each one interacts with the others to help or hinder the child's progress at home and at school. To give just one example: being able to make a friend (social development) can give a child confidence to do what the friend does, an important step in building the child's self-esteem (emotional development). If the shared activity is climbing on the frame, this helps physical/motor development. As the children plan how to construct a sequence of movement (what comes first, then next and how does it all finish?) in a way which adapts to suit a particular context, their creative and aesthetic development and their knowledge and understanding of the world is boosted.

Although many curriculum documents combine issues under the umbrella term, 'emotional, personal and social development' (EPSD), each element is considered separately in this introductory section because each has important elements which might just be obscured in a combined framework. Gaining confidence is part of emotional development and if this does not progress then the reason why has to be discovered. Looking at the outcome, e.g. that the child fails to answer questions about events in a story, may need to have the underlying reason explored rather than giving more practice in answering questions. This could be a lack of confidence to speak out in front of friends; a lack of experience in listening to stories so the child loses the plot; or lack of ability to concentrate or pay attention rather than the intellectual deficit of 'not understanding' the story itself.

Emotional development

This is closely allied to social development but focuses on the affective or the feeling states such as altruism and empathy. It concerns children:

- having the confidence to stay at nursery;
- being able to approach new learning activities confidently;
- having a positive self-esteem;
- being able to join in groups to work and play;
- developing altruism, i.e. caring for others;
- developing empathy, i.e. being able to appreciate how others are feeling and acting towards them sympathetically.

Stories about other children or pets or fairy tales can all help emotional development if the discussion following the story helps the children to empathise, i.e. to understand other people's feelings, e.g. 'How did baby bear feel when he saw his chair was broken or that his porridge was all eaten up?' or 'When you bring a new pet home, how will it feel?' Through sharing interactions like this, children realise that others feel emotions just like themselves and so they come to respect their point of view. They also come to realise that it's alright being afraid at times and that it is helpful to explain rather than bottle up negative feelings which tend to grow.

If the children don't learn to empathise with others, their potential for making friends will be reduced. At first, the three-year-olds will tend to be caught up in their own lives rather than being concerned as to how others are feeling, but gradually this passes. By the time they are approaching four, they are beginning to appreciate how their own behaviour affects others, so this could be the best time to introduce 'helping others' as a theme.

Social and personal development

Through social development, the children learn to make friends, to share, to take turns, to co-operate with others, to appreciate that others have different points of view and may want to do different things. They also learn how to talk with their friends and with adults (who may want a more mannerly approach!) and learn to listen. Many teachers and parents consider that until the children are socially competent their learning can be hindered.

All of these are promoted in the nursery activities where the staff are looking out to encourage and support each child.

Helping a child to make friends

Sometimes children are reluctant to join in or, for any number of reasons, they are left on the outside of a group. One strategy which has been shown to help is to find the child's particular interests – perhaps from chatting with the child or asking the parents, 'What does he or she really like to do?' and set up an activity based on the answer. Then the staff can think of one or two children with similar interests and encourage them to join in. The child who is familiar with the activity (the one who has necessitated all this planning) should be able to make some contribution which will hopefully act as an icebreaker. If the staff predict that this might not happen because the child is unsure, then some preliminary time spent discussing ideas could help.

Social activities in the nursery include:

- gathering together at story time;
- waiting to take their turn on the climbing frame;
- making dough together – one measuring, one stirring, one pouring;
- role play – mums and dads in the house corner, nurses and doctors in the hospital corner; cooperative building in the construction corner etc.;
- making snack for the other children;
- sitting at the table together, passing plates etc.;
- washing up after snack.

All of these help to develop life skills which will enable children to interact appropriately in different contexts.

Knowledge and understanding of the world (K & U)

This is implicit in every activity, although initially parents may tend to think about reading, writing and counting. These are important, ongoing activities which feature in the nursery every day in a child-centred way, but parents have to be helped to recognise the varied learning within the many opportunities that are offered and understand that these are planned to match and enhance the developmental level of their children. The children learn about many aspects of their world – cultural aspects as well as how to become more proficient in all the activities of daily living. In that way they are helped to become more independent learners.

Early listening and talking skills are encouraged as well as the first stages in writing and counting. Recognition of sounds – orally then with accompanying symbols – precedes reading and the children enjoy stories and poems specially chosen for their age group.

The children develop intellectually through many hands-on practical activities. They learn, for example, about:

- the texture of different materials and their uses, e.g. waterproof clothing;
- the changing properties of objects under different conditions, e.g. ice melting and water solidifying;
- how the environment and their own lifestyles are affected by the weather;
- foods which are healthy and provide warmth and energy, e.g. soup and porridge;
- how animals and birds survive the winter;
- how the weather varies in different lands (from personal experience or stories, or TV programmes);
- the different kinds of work people do.

Physical/motor development (Phys)

Much of the learning in the nursery is hands-on, where children feel the properties of objects and handle them so that they retain what they have learned. They also have the freedom to move around and are encouraged to develop their basic movement patterns, e.g. crawling, walking, running, hopping, jumping – and all combinations of these. Progress can depend on their coordination, balance and dexterity. These are very important competencies because movement is a healthy thing to enjoy. It lets children join in games with their friends and gives them confidence to become involved in many leisure activities. Moreover, movement underpins much early learning as shown below.

Fine motor skills are required (dependent on dexterity and coordination) in activities such as painting, cutting, threading, gluing and baking, drawing and writing. They are also needed for fastening buttons, tying aprons, serving a snack, drinking through a straw and many other daily activities.

Gross motor skills are required for all the simple and combined basic movement patterns, e.g. crawling, walking, running, climbing, hopping and skipping – and the combinations of patterns such as running and jumping. These are dependent on the movement abilities of coordination, balance, rhythm and timing, and being able to use the correct amount of strength and speed.

Manipulative skills are required when controlling an object. They allow children to stir a mixture with one hand while holding a bowl with the other; to hold a piece of macaroni steady with one hand while threading raffia through it with the other; to use a bat and ball together with some success. These skills depend on hand–eye coordination, timing and tracking as well as being able to use the correct amount of strength and speed.

From the very earliest days, children's progress is monitored by observing their motor skills, e.g. when they hold up their heads; when they sit up unsupported; when they walk; if they crawl; when they use the pincer grip to lift and replace objects. These motor milestones are the first recorded observations which gauge children's progress. There is a normative time for these kinds of competencies to be achieved and nursery staff have to understand these stages so that they may recognise the children's stage of development and take steps to provide challenges or reinforcements to ensure progress. (For a full list of competences, see Ch. 3, p. 22.)

Sensory perception

One important aspect which underlies all of the headings is perception, i.e. how children take cues from the environment through the different senses to guide them in the things they wish to do. How do the senses impact on learning?

Vestibular sense

This sense influences balance which is intrinsic to every movement and even plays a large part in the ability to be still. Children who have a poorly developed vestibular sense are often described as awkward and/or restless as they fight to gain the control which other children take for granted.

Visual sense

This is the functional side of seeing. Children use it to track words in books and older children need it to copy from the board. It is also necessary in following the path of a ball and explains why some children find catching one so difficult. Like vestibular sense, it contributes to balance. Children with reading difficulties should have their functional vision checked. In the nursery, staff should look out for children who close one eye or hold their heads at a strange angle when 'reading' a book for they may need early expert help to correct a visual difficulty.

Auditory sense

How often do parents and teachers complain about children who 'don't listen'? The reason can be more complicated than just not paying attention for there are many children who have difficulty with the level of their hearing. Some children have auditory distractibility which means that they are distracted by the least rustle. They then leave what they are doing to go to investigate! They may genuinely not hear what the teacher or parent has to say because they can't cut out other noises. Some children will find the pitch of certain sounds intolerable and to cope they shut out all the other sounds around them. This may be the reason why they may appear withdrawn.

Proprioceptive sense

The proprioceptors are nerve endings in the skin which relay positional information to the brain. If children appear clumsy, there are games that help to develop body awareness, help them to recognise where their body parts are and where they end and the outside world begins. This is essential for precise movement. Lots of 'Simon Says' type games or songs such as 'Heads, Shoulders, Knees and Toes' are very helpful in developing this sense. Teachers should include elbows and backs because sometimes children aren't too sure they are there!

Kinaesthetic sense

This sense helps children know where they are functioning in space. Spatial perception is a fundamental ability that allows children to appreciate the distance between objects as well as how far they themselves are from them. Making incorrect judgements means that movements are clumsy with many spills and falls.

Sense of taste

Children are given the opportunity to taste many unusual and exotic foods in the nursery. Even if some are unwilling to taste, they can still learn about the size, the shape, the texture and the smell of the items.

Keith has planted hyacinths. Later he will discover that they give a lovely smell.

Many sensory activities can cross themes to give varied experiences. The example given here concerns the sense of smell.

Sense of smell

It is helpful if the children's sense of smell can be developed as this sense also helps their spatial orientation. It can also warn them of danger, e.g. that something is burning. How can this be done? Activities across the nursery can be used to introduce different scents, e.g.:

- add peppermint flavouring to the dough and ask the children to identify the smell –the colour and texture do not change;
- put orange- or lime-scented soap in the toilets;
- bring in a bowl of hyacinths or freesias;
- add coconut essence when baking biscuits;
- add scented baby bath to the water tray;
- use grapefruit-scented washing-up liquid in the snack area.

A 'guess the smell' game can be made very simply by putting pieces of sponge into empty film canisters and adding vinegar, vanilla essence, strawberry essence etc. The lids stay on until the children unscrew them; the challenge is to 'guess the smells!'

Cloves and lavender can be added to the gluing table along with dried, shredded citrus peel; make egg sandwiches for snack; a tray of aromatic herbs allows children to rub the plants and release new smells – there are lots of fun ways to help children appreciate the different scents in their environment.

Lavender bags are easy to make and make lovely gifts to take home. 'Making a present' for the person coming to collect the child reassures him or her that this will happen and so helps them to settle. (See Ch. 5, p. 75 for the different stages in making lavender bags.)

All of these different aspects contribute to the development of the 'whole child'. This very brief introduction to each of them indicates how skilled nursery staff have to be in observing their children, recognising their strengths and their difficulties and knowing how to support them in these very important learning days. They also have to help many parents to do this too (for details on observation, assessment and recording see Ch. 6, p. 91).

3 Planning and organising in the nursery

The year plan based on the natural calendar

Using the 'natural calendar' is a sound way to begin a year plan because the format gives an immediate visual picture of what is happening when. While some topics are prescribed, most depend on the interests the children reveal. Staff have to consider the ethnic and religious diversity in their nursery and local community as they select the prescribed topics for the plan to ensure that each group of children enjoys input that is important to their culture. At an early stage, this forward plan can be shared with parents to help keep them involved in their children's learning. The plan also gives notice of any resources that have to be gathered or 'outside people' who have to be contacted and given sufficient notice to allow the anticipated activities to take place.

Year plans also allow comparisons and evaluations over time as to what worked well, what was disappointing and what amendments might be needed before trying out a topic again. Planning over two years allows a considerable number of topics to be introduced and some may be revisited to allow for reinforcement or extension work, i.e. using a spiral curriculum. In this way the year plan provides a dynamic record of events which shows that the full curriculum is being offered to the children. Constant reference is made to the curriculum documents to ensure that the appropriate learning outcomes are all covered; continual evaluation by the staff will ensure that the best ways to achieve them are planned. This requires the learning demands to be correctly matched to the children's level of development. The year plan could also be shared with other staff during the transition process to 'big school' to help them appreciate the kinds of learning activities the children have experienced and enjoyed at this earlier stage.

Of course, this is not the whole story. There are skills and understandings which the children need to have to allow them to cope at home and at school, e.g. being able to dress and undress independently or being able to spread butter on their toast. It is possible that there are only a few children who have not acquired such skills or not been given the opportunity to practise them, so they may not arise naturally as choices within a child-centred framework. However, staff should ensure that all of these life skills or activities of daily living or special cultural events are all covered in a logical sequence throughout the time (usually two years) that the children spend in their preschool setting. This should provide a solid foundation for the children's transition to the next stage.

Anticipating children's interests

Through experience, it is possible to anticipate topics which are very likely to be initiated by the children. This means that resources can be built up over time so that they can be 'produced' at the right moment! If some examples of these are listed near the year plan, they can be ticked off as they are chosen by the children thus providing a complete record of the children's experiences.

	Emotional, Personal & Social Development	Communication & Language	Knowledge & Understanding of the World	Expressive & Aesthetic (Creative) Development	Physical Development & Movement
AUGUST	Myself at Nursery Handwashing campaign		Fruit and Veg 2D Shape	Printing (Fruit and Veg)	Climbing (Outdoor Equipment)
SEPTEMBER	"	Traditional tales	"	"	Crawling check "
OCTOBER			Farm Animals Colours	Begin to use Jingle Time (see Bibliography)	Sponsored Obstacle Course
NOVEMBER		Sequencing Days of the Week	Autumn		Movement in the Gym
DECEMBER	Christmas			Clay Craft Decorations	Spatial Awareness
JANUARY	Burns Night Chinese New Year	Introduce Story Sacks (Sound Lotto Games)	Winter		Moving on Different Parts of the Body
FEBRUARY	Personal Safety		People Who Help Us	Role Play (People who help us)	Ball & Bean Bag Skill
MARCH	Easter/New Life		My Body/Growth		Balancing
APRIL	"		Numeracy Butterfly Farm		Fine Motor Skills
MAY		Auditory Discrimination Alphabet Awareness	Life Cycles (Minibeasts)		
JUNE	School Playground Visits	School	Sea Life	Expr & Aesth Activities Integrated with Other Topics	

Spanning labels: POETRY AND RHYME (Communication & Language), COMPUTER (Knowledge & Understanding of the World), MATHEMATICAL LANGUAGE (Expressive & Aesthetic Development)

Note: Cultural festivals as appropriate to children in the nursery

Figure 3.1 The year plan based on the natural calendar

Children's interests with ideas to develop discussions

- **Babies** – new baby at home, caring (feeding, dressing, soothing), what babies can/cannot do, where and how long they sleep, family relationships.
- **Weddings** – bride and groom, bridesmaids and ushers, guests, dresses, kilts or ethnic costumes as appropriate, making invitations, wedding cakes, other special food, going on honeymoon. The wedding ceremony, flowers, minister, vicar or registrar, organ music.
- **Hospitals** – nurses and doctors, stethoscope, X-ray machines, medicines, bandages. Ambulances and paramedics, stretchers. Visitors and treats, getting better, going home.
- **People who help us** – childminders, lollipop men/women, police officers, nurses and doctors, plumbers etc.
- **Transport** – trains, buses, coaches, cars, aircraft, barges, long boats etc.
- **The farm** – animals, crops, dairy produce. Machinery – tractors, milking machines.
- **The zoo** – exotic animals, snakes and birds. Living conditions: why these creatures would not be suitable as a pet.
- **Starting school** – getting a school bag, a lunchbox, a pencil case. Meeting a new teacher and making new friends. Learning new things. Travelling to school etc. (see also Ch. 7, 'Transitions').

The amount of detail should be appropriate for the level of interest and the children's experiences. All the issues arising from the interests should be dealt with in a positive way and opportunities to develop them should not be missed, e.g. road crossings exist so that children and old people will not be hurt crossing the road. Do the children know where their local crossings are? How do people know when to cross? (Stress that the children should never cross the road without an adult.)

Similarly, children should be taught that X-ray machines take magic pictures just like an ordinary camera – they don't hurt. The children's department in a local hospital might part with one or two plates of the types of fractures experienced by children, e.g. arms and ankles, to help children learn about their own bone structure as well as learning how to take care of themselves. All these ideas and many others can be the source of much worthwhile learning if staff just remember to see everything through the children's eyes!

The year plan, therefore, is an amalgam of pre-set learning and opportunities for the children's interests to be followed. Some flexibility should be built in to allow themes or interests that continue for longer than anticipated to be followed through. There are also times when learning opportunities may close down rather early; staff should recognise when this happens and discuss the reasons why at their evaluation meetings.

The term diary: a term at a glance

The term diary is an instant reference document which should be displayed on the staff notice board. Staff should record all the special events known at the start of term and add others as they arise. Items are likely to include the following:

Inspection dates

Visitors to the nursery

Holidays and cultural festivals

In-service days/staff meetings (an asterisk can indicate that staff cover has to be arranged)

The staff rota, i.e. the area and times of each member of staff's responsibilities

Children arriving for the first time (new starts)

Children's birthdays

Date	Rota of staff responsibilities	Monday	Tuesday	Wednesday	Thursday Library Day	Friday
6–10 January	Areas 1 – Anne 2 – Jo 3 – Fred	Holiday ✕ 6	In-service am – course (music) pm – list needs 7	8	Resources from ???? arriving 9	10
13–17 January	Areas 1 – Fred 2 – Anne 3 – Jo	David's birthday (4) 13	14	9.30–10.30 Zainab New Start 15	16	Arrange farm visit, book minibus 17
20–24 January	Areas 1 – Jo 2 – Fred 3 – Anne	Librarian (story) 20	21	Anna T New Start 1–2 22	Multi-agency meeting re Sam starting school 23	Burns Day (25th) 24
*Student 27–31 January	Areas 1 – Anne 2 – Jo 3 – Fred	Collect money (farm trip – £1) 27	Meet Asha's psychologist 28	29	Parents' meeting (4-year-olds) 30	31
*Student 3–7 February	Areas 1 – Fred 2 – Anne 3 – Jo	Mid-term break ✕ 3	Letter to helpers (farm visit) 4	Buy supplies for trip. Complete student profile 5	6	Check displays: records 7
*Student 10–14 February	Areas 1 – Jo 2 – Fred 3 – Anne	10	Check mobiles, first-aid kits 11	Trip to farm 12	13	14
17–21 February	Areas 1 – Anne 2 – Jo 3 – Fred	← 17	Inspection ← ↕ → 18	→ 19	Staff meeting 3.30–5.30 20	21
24–28 February	Areas 1 – Fred 2 – Anne 3 – Jo	Liam's birthday (5) 24	Meet new parents Emma & John 25	26	27	St David's Day (1 March) 28
3–7 March	Areas 1 – Jo 2 – Fred 3 – Anne	Contact primary re transition 3	4	5	6	In-service (Jo & Anne) Cover required 7
10–14 March	Areas 1 – Anne 2 – Jo 3 – Fred	10	11	Transition meeting 12	13	Shop for St Patrick's Day 14

Code: **Area 1:** water, sand, paint, glue, dough, clay; **Area 2:** snack, baking, computer, puzzle, construction; **Area 3:** house, book corner, story, outdoors
*Student from college   ✕ = Holiday

Figure 3.2 The staff diary: a term at a glance

Trips and outings

Any other reminders of important and/or unusual events

Reminders to order resources which take time to arrive

The monthly plan

The monthly plan may include several different topics taken from the year plan, but some issues will have been anticipated and necessary arrangements put in place prior to this time. These and all the other happenings for each of the weeks within the month should be discussed at the monthly planning meeting.

One way to ease planning is to gather the targets or competences from the relevant curriculum document and arrange these in lists for quick and easy reference (see Fig. 3.3). Thereafter the key competences from each aspect which are appropriate to each theme can be identified. As the themes or topics change, the lists can show how the competences are being covered, ensuring a balanced planning approach. Examples are shown in Figure 3.4.

Organisational responsibilities are then allocated to staff, e.g.:

- ordering resources;
- planning outings;
- organising staff cover for staff development days;
- considering what communications need to be sent to parents;
- planning and preparing notices for the staff notice board;
- checking up on the arrival of students and allocating time to support them;
- arranging afternoon and evening meetings for the parents to come in to hear about their children's progress;
- fund-raising ideas and plans for making them happen.

Nursery areas are allocated to staff. Once these have been allocated, the staff begin to consider the detail of the activities they will provide or lead each week. They have to know the different kinds of learning which can happen in each area (see Figs 3.6–3.13) and the ways in which these can be promoted or adapted to complement the current topic.

This ongoing preparation and continual discussion among the staff eliminates the need for a regular weekly meeting – although one can be called if a crisis arises!

The daily plan or the nursery day

A typical nursery day

8.30am–9.00am: setting up. Staff gather for a recap of children who need special attention and the kind of support they require, e.g.:

'Kieran has a new inhaler – collect it from his mum – look out for any reaction.'

'Alison's second short visit. She is coming at 9.30am with her childminder who will stay until Alison settles. She will then go off for about an hour. Staff look out for her return and be ready to unlock the door.'

Staff check the daily plan and if necessary the term diary. This reminds them of their particular responsibilities for each part of the day, e.g. their 'special children' for observing and recording progress/regression and which areas they are covering. For their own area of responsibility, staff check:

EPSD	Communication	Knowledge & Understanding	Creative & Expressive Development	Physical Development & Movement
1. Develop confidence, self-esteem and a sense of security.	1. Have fun with language and making stories.	1. Develop their powers of observation using their senses.	1. Investigate and use a variety of media and techniques such as painting, drawing, printing and modelling with fabrics, clay and other materials.	1. Enjoy energetic activity both indoors and out and the feeling of well-being that it brings.
2. Care for themselves and their personal safety.	2. Listen to other children and adults during social activities and play.	2. Recognise patterns, shapes and colours in the world around them.	2. Express thoughts and feelings in pictures, paintings and models.	2. Explore different ways in which they can use their bodies in physical activity.
3. Develop independence, e.g. in dressing and personal hygiene.	3. Listen with enjoyment and respond to stories, songs, music, rhymes and other poetry.	3. Sort and categorise things into groups.	3. Use role play or puppets to recreate and invent situations.	3. Use their bodies to express ideas and feelings in response to music and imaginative ideas.
4. Persevere in tasks that at first present some difficulties.	4. Listen and respond to the sounds and rhythm of words in stories, songs, music and rhymes.	4. Understand some properties of materials, e.g. soft/hard, smooth/rough.	4. Use verbal and non-verbal language in role play.	4. Run, jump, skip, climb, balance, throw and catch with increasing skill and confidence.
5. Express appropriately feelings, needs and preferences.	5. Pay attention to information and instructions from an adult.	5. Understand the routines and jobs of familiar people.	5. Listen and respond to sounds, rhythms, songs and a variety of music.	5. Cooperate with others in physical play and games.
6. Form positive relationships with other children and adults, and begin to develop particular friendships with other children.	6. Talk to other children or with an adult about themselves and their experiences.	6. Become familiar with the early years setting and places in the local area.	6. Make music by singing, clapping and playing percussion instruments.	6. Develop increasing control of the fine movements of their fingers and hands.
7. Become aware of and respect the needs and feelings of others in their behaviour, and learn to follow rules.	7. Express needs, thoughts and feelings with increasing confidence in speech and non-verbal language.	7. Become aware of everyday uses of technology and use these appropriately (scissors, water-proof clothing, fridge, bicycle).	7. Use instruments by themselves and in groups to invent music that expresses their thoughts and feelings.	7. Develop awareness of space.
8. Make and express choices, plans and decisions.	8. Take part in short and more extended conversations.	8. Be aware of daily time sequences and words to describe/measure time, e.g. snack time, morning, first, next, clock.	8. Move rhythmically and expressively to music.	8. Be safe in movement and in using tools and equipment.
9. Play cooperatively, take turns and share resources.	9. Use talk during role play and re-tell a story or rhyme.	9. Be aware of change and its effects on them, e.g. their own growth, changes in weather, trees, flowers.	9. Participate in simple dances and singing games.	9. Be aware of the importance of health and fitness.
10. Become aware that the celebration of cultural and religious festivals is important in people's lives.	10. Use language for a variety of purposes, e.g. to describe, explain, predict, ask questions and develop ideas.	10. Care for living things, e.g. pets at home.		
11. Develop positive attitudes towards others whose gender, language, religion or culture, for example, is different from their own.	11. Use books to find interesting information.	11. Be aware of feeling good and of the importance of hygiene, diet, exercise and personal safety.		
12. Care for the environment and for other people in the community.	12. Recognise the link between the written and spoken word.	12. Develop an appreciation of natural beauty and a sense of wonder about the world.		
	13. Understand some of the language and layout of books.	13. Understand and use mathematical processes such as matching, grouping, counting and measuring.		
	14. Develop an awareness of letter names and sounds in the context of play experiences.	14. Apply these processes in solving mathematical problems.		
	15. Use their own drawings and written marks to express ideas and feelings.	15. Identify and use numbers up to ten during play experiences and counting games.		
	16. Experiment with symbols, letters and, in some cases, words in writing.	16. Recognise familiar shapes during play activities.		
	17. Recognise some familiar words and letters, e.g. the initial letter in their name.	17. Use mathematical language appropriate to the learning situations.		

Figure 3.3 Lists of learning outcomes/competences from the Curriculum Framework 3–5

EPSD	Communication	Knowledge & Understanding	Creative & Expressive Development	Physical Development & Movement
Winter theme	**Winter theme**	**Winter theme**	**Winter theme**	**Winter theme**
3 & 4 Dressing for outside – gloves, boots, hats, zips and scarves.	**3, 4, 13** Lots of winter stories and poems.	**1, 4, 7, 12** Ice, snow, textures and temperatures. Use freezer to make ice, melt indoors, add colour and freeze then melt again in the water tray.	**1** Investigate the effect of white paint on black paper.	**1** Outdoor play – discuss energy level and keeping warm.
9 Cooperating to make a snowman.	**2, 6, 7, 10** Interacting and planning to build a snowman together.	**9** Use bubbles in the garden to show wind speed and direction.	**2** Discuss the effect of the wind – how do the children feel when there is a gale?	**5** Cooperating to clear the snow shovelling, filling wheelbarrows with snow, rolling snow for snowman.
1 Use a large box. Make a black sugar paper door flap. Provide a torch. Children may feel brave enough to sit inside, switch off the torch and experience total darkness.		**10** Make bird cake for the birds.	On windy days make kites and discuss what shapes help the kites to stay up.	**8** Safety in using tools – awareness of space between bodies.
		15, 17 Count buttons on the snowman, the number of birds who eat the bird cake.	**3 & 4** Provide winter clothes for dressing the dolls.	
		17 Discuss the weight of the ice.	**9** Have a Jack Frost dance where fingers become icicles.	
The Chinese New Year theme	**The Chinese New Year theme**	**The Chinese New Year theme**	**The Chinese New Year theme**	**The Chinese New Year theme**
10 & 11 How Chinese people celebrate the New Year.	**3 & 13** Use dual language books.	**7** Cooking; use Chinese ingredients: noodles, beansprouts, etc. taste raw.	**1** Provide fine paintbrushes. Posters with Chinese script.	**8** Safe use of knives when chopping veg for stir fry.
Which animal this year? What do they eat/wear? How do they decorate their homes?	**1 & 9** The Chinese New Year story.	Display for 1 day, cook the next.	**2** Provide strips of egg boxes to suggest the Chinese dragon.	**6** Provide chopsticks to allow children to try.
Lucky money bags.	**1 & 11** Make lion puppet. (2 lollipop sticks, circle for face, wool for mane. Folded paper for body – use sticks to make puppet move.)	Tasting session lychees.	**3** Provide traditional costumes.	**5** Moving the lion/dragon puppet rhythmically to the music.
Make or buy bags.		Peelings can go on gluing table.	**5** Play tape of Chinese music.	
Make coin-sized biscuits (shape biscuits, recipe P).				

Figure 3.4 This selection of competences is highlighted in the Winter and Chinese New Year themes

Source/Observation	Content	Support for Learning	Possible Learning Outcomes	Key Aspect	Evaluation
Snow lying in the garden	Outside	Open outdoor area for those who wish to go out. Fill water tray with snow for others	Experience sun on snow. Snow handling – texture; temperature. Learn through experience that snow melts with heat and turns to water	Knowledge and understanding	See below
Children needing support/encouragement to dress properly for garden/outdoors/going home	Cloakroom	Encourage self-help in fastening coats, putting on hats, scarves	Understand need for woolly gloves – waterproof coats. Able to fasten coats	EPSD Physical/ Motor development	Children impatient to go outside. Fastening buttons very difficult (Zoe, Tim, Lewis)
3-year-olds coping well with Sound Lotto game (same sound)	Puzzle table	Introduce new Lotto game – each child has different picture this time	Children have to listen and identify their own sounds – different from their neighbours	Communication and language and EPSD	John, Freya and Reena coping well. Encourage Tim to stay on task.
Several children finding spreading difficult	Snack	Provide ingredients for banana sandwiches and recipe book	Follow picture instructions. Safe use of knife. Increase in skill	Physical/Motor	Spreading improving – try toast and cheese spread

Evaluation and next steps: Morning group

Outdoors: Crisp snow – children made snowballs and cooperated in making a snowman. Experienced packing snow together – change of texture.
Carol found stones and counted out buttons correctly.
Most preschoolers managed coats and hats but not gloves. *Work on hand awareness with 3-year-old group. Incy Wincy Spider. Adam and Bradley can't manage zips (check hand dominance). Good link with snowman video.

Evaluation and next steps: Afternoon group

Indoors: Snow in water tray melting – discuss what is happening – where the water comes from. Leave until morning – refreeze some.
Sounds Lotto game: Liam, Alex, Ginny need support.
Banana sandwiches: Spreading improving – try toast and cheese spread tomorrow.
Alanna settling down. Not yet willing to go outside.

Figure 3.5 The daily plan and evaluation

- that all the resources are ready (pencils sharpened, water filled up etc.);
- that name sheets are available;
- that the area is tidy;
- the layout and variety of items which are provided;
- their suitability for the developmental level of the children.

Staff also have to gauge when additions have to be made to existing resources to stimulate further interest or when resources have outlived their usefulness and need to be changed.

The positioning/spacing of their own areas should be examined, e.g. will the passage of children disrupt the gluing activity? Can staff oversee their 'second' area of responsibility while seated at the first? If not, they have to plan how the areas could be rearranged to allow for this. It should be noted that the layout of the different areas can influence the children's behaviour, e.g. too much clear space ahead can encourage running! On the other hand access to the fire doors must be kept free, so planning the total spatial environment helps to ensure the smooth running of the nursery. The outdoor apparatus should be set up and checked for safety.

Staff check on their own break times from the daily plan and also how the changeover of supervision and teaching will be affected. If the member of staff on snack takes the last break, as just one example, the baking will be ready for sharing at celebration time or going home! There must be no gaps in the staffing of the outdoor area as this would be a danger to the children, so this has to be carefully organised.

9.00am: the doors open. One member of staff welcomes the children and their carers, offers support to any child who may be reluctant to stay and at the same time polices the door to make absolutely sure no children slip out. (Doors must be safety-locked at either end of the sessions.) Parents must recognise the danger if they leave an outside door open and stand chatting to other mums or dads – they have to come in or stay out!

The register should be available near the door so that parents can sign in their child. They must also record if any other person is authorised to collect their child. A name and phone number for this other person is essential to prevent forgotten children feeling abandoned because no one knows who Auntie Susie is, or where she can be found! This is in addition to any verbal information passed to staff.

Some nurseries make a child-sized copy of the register and as the children arrive, they tick their own names off. While this is good name recognition practice, unless there is plenty of room near the door, it may cause delay and prevent others getting in.

Neither of these records can substitute for the staff carefully checking the register at each session. Parents can forget to sign their child in or they may sign in the wrong place so the member of staff who has been allocated register responsibility must make a careful, final head count. Accurate registers for each session are essential for safety, e.g. fire drill.

9.00am onwards: free flow play at the various areas (see Ch. 5 for details of activities). Staff observe and record both the level and quality of the children's participation, evaluate the provision at their special areas and evaluate their own participation.

They observe and make appropriate recordings about:

- what the children choose to do;
- how well they cope (share, talk, stay involved, complete work);
- what sort of extension or reinforcement each child needs and how this is to be carried out;
- whether the area holds the children's interest;
- what other resources could be substituted or added.

Self-evaluation is ongoing too because getting it right is not easy. Staff should note things to discuss at the end of session meeting such as reflections on:

- were they able to make their planned observations or were they distracted, and if so how can this be overcome?
- were they able to extend the children's talk and if not, what advice would other staff give?
- did they intervene appropriately or stay back?
- was this effective and if not, what else could be done?

(See Ch. 4 for more detail on observation, assessment and recording.)
   During this time staff are carrying out the organisational plan. This involves:

- covering for other staff as they take their break;
- checking that by 10.30am all children have had the opportunity for a snack;
- checking that any medication has been given;
- providing planned activities.

10.45am: the staff supervise the children's tidy-up time. Children should wash paint brushes, sweep up sand, put toys and dishes, pots and pans and construction equipment all away in the correct places (many of these can be colour coded or have the shape of the item drawn on the shelf to ease placement). Tidying up is much more efficient if it is phrased as a reward, e.g. 'Who has worked really hard today? I'm going to let them sweep up the sand!' Commands such as 'Who spilt that sand – get it tidied up' do not promote cooperation and may even start off arguments as it is usually 'someone else' who has made the mess!

10.55am: if there is birthday cake to share or baking to taste, everyone comes together for a short time before 'Story'.

11.05am: children gather in their groups for story.

11.20am: all the children come together with one member of staff who leads singing. While this is going on, the other staff empty and refill the water tray, replenish any resources, check the security of heavy equipment and rewash dishes at the snack area ready for the next group of children. One member of staff is on door duty to greet the parents while another sets out the lunch tables for the full-time children.

11.30am: the morning group should have left; full-timers wash their hands ready for lunch.

11.35am: one member of staff supervises lunch; ideally an auxiliary, otherwise the member of staff may miss the evaluation meeting.

11.30am–11.45am: the daily meeting is held to 'evaluate today and plan for tomorrow'. At the meeting, staff:

- discuss individual children's progress and share suggestions/strategies to offer extension or reinforcement;
- evaluate the provision and discuss changes;
- share any child's interest that is not part of the immediate plan and discuss how to include it;
- consult the weekly plan to check provision and responsibilities for tomorrow.

   One 8.30am–9.00am preparation time each week is allocated to keeping the assessment records up to date, e.g. inserting the sticky labels (taken from a roll) or the field notes into the correct file, collating and analysing these observations. From the results, some amendments in the plan may be made (for details about recording observations on sticky labels see Ch. 6, p. 91).

The programme in the afternoon follows the same format.

Sometimes there is a gap between the end of lunch and the arrival of the afternoon children. This means that the full-timers require some 'other' activity such as playing out of doors, listening to a story tape or some music time. If possible the nursery should be left tidy for the afternoon set of children. This is more welcoming and gives the children the chance to begin a game rather than having to join in one that is already up and running; it also gives all the children a chance to learn about routines and sequencing, i.e. what comes first, then next. This helps their planning and organising abilities.

Learning in the different areas of the nursery

The nursery has several basic areas which are the foundations of learning, e.g. snack; the house corner; water and sand; music; outdoor play on large apparatus; large and small construction areas; the garden and the outdoor environment; puzzles and jigsaws; painting, gluing and craft (see Figs 3.6–3.13). Suggestions for activities which enhance learning in these basic areas are detailed in Chapter 3.

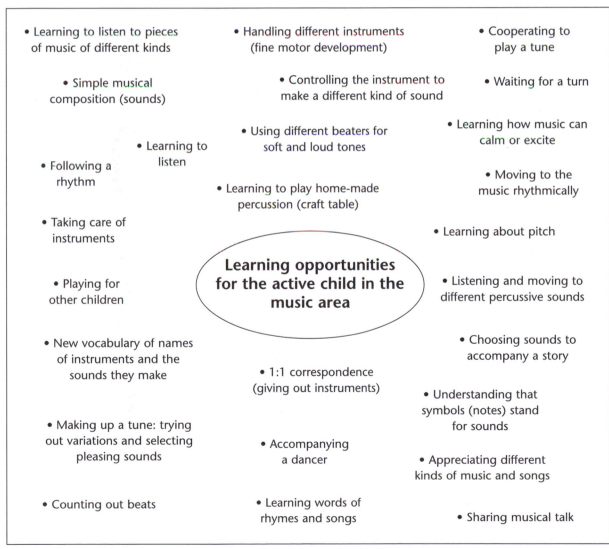

Figure 3.6 Learning opportunities for the active child in the music area

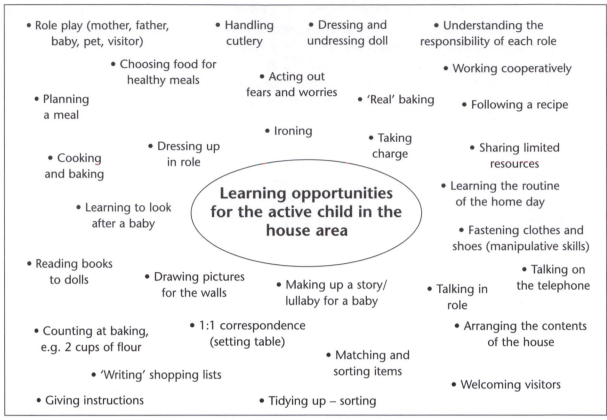

Figure 3.7 Learning opportunities for the active child in the house area

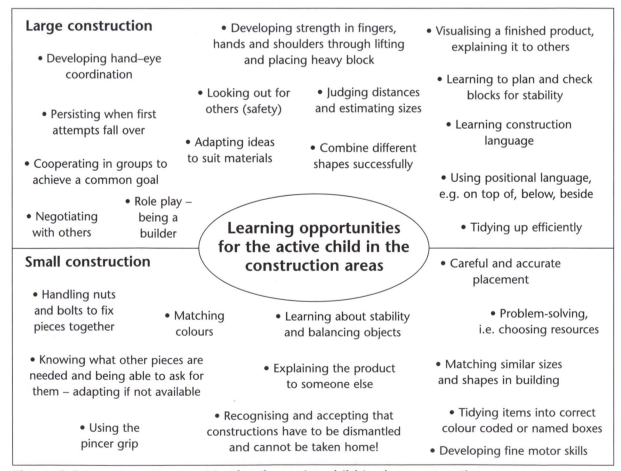

Figure 3.8 Learning opportunities for the active child in the construction areas

Figure 3.9 Learning opportunities for the active child in the outdoor large apparatus area

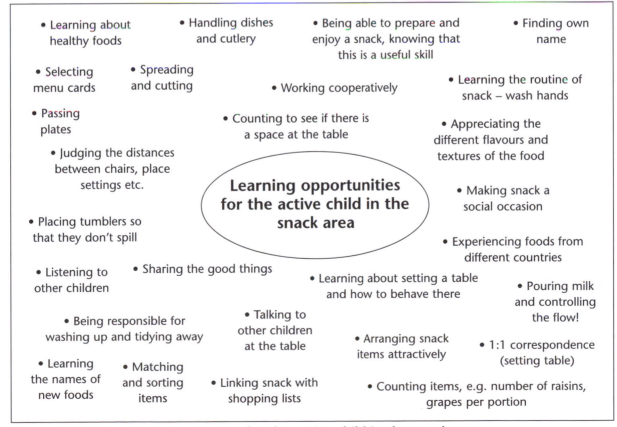

Figure 3.10 Learning opportunities for the active child in the snack area

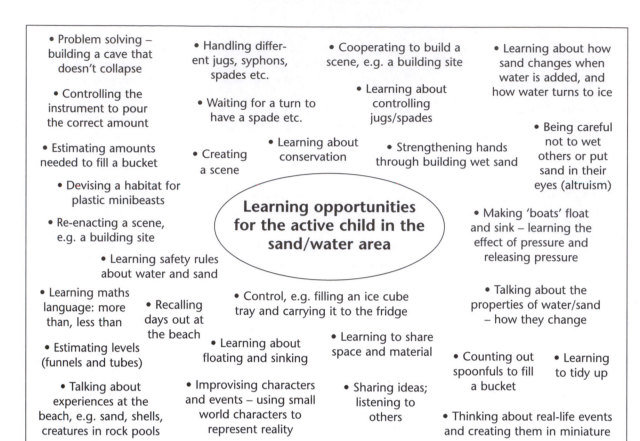

Figure 3.11 Learning opportunities for the active child in the sand/water area

Figure 3.12 Learning opportunities for the active child in the garden/outdoor area

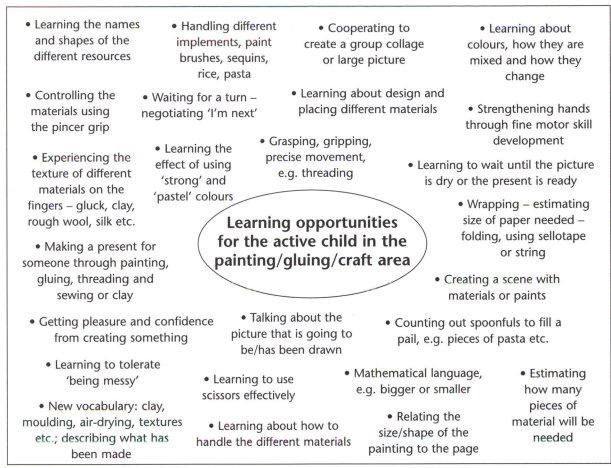

- Learning the names and shapes of the different resources
- Handling different implements, paint brushes, sequins, rice, pasta
- Cooperating to create a group collage or large picture
- Learning about colours, how they are mixed and how they change
- Controlling the materials using the pincer grip
- Waiting for a turn – negotiating 'I'm next'
- Learning about design and placing different materials
- Strengthening hands through fine motor skill development
- Experiencing the texture of different materials on the fingers – gluck, clay, rough wool, silk etc.
- Learning the effect of using 'strong' and 'pastel' colours
- Grasping, gripping, precise movement, e.g. threading
- Learning to wait until the picture is dry or the present is ready

Learning opportunities for the active child in the painting/gluing/craft area

- Wrapping – estimating size of paper needed – folding, using sellotape or string
- Making a present for someone through painting, gluing, threading and sewing or clay
- Creating a scene with materials or paints
- Getting pleasure and confidence from creating something
- Talking about the picture that is going to be/has been drawn
- Counting out spoonfuls to fill a pail, e.g. pieces of pasta etc.
- Learning to tolerate 'being messy'
- Learning to use scissors effectively
- Mathematical language, e.g. bigger or smaller
- Estimating how many pieces of material will be needed
- New vocabulary: clay, moulding, air-drying, textures etc.; describing what has been made
- Learning about how to handle the different materials
- Relating the size/shape of the painting to the page

Figure 3.13 Learning opportunities for the active child in the painting/gluing/craft area

Adapting the basic areas

These basic areas can quickly be adapted to follow the children's interests and extend their play. The shop can become a café, the house corner a hospital and the outside play area can encourage planting seeds and learning about habitats as well as developing gross motor skills on large apparatus. The possibilities for development are endless if they can be resourced, but they should stay true to the children's interests rather than producing showpieces for visitors. It makes sense to develop these interests at the most appropriate time, e.g. 'going to big school' should obviously happen near transition time (for more information see Ch. 7).

Adapting the areas can have another important function such as relieving children's worries (see below).

Children's worries

Parents will often explain that their child is worried about going to the dentist or to hospital for an operation. On the other hand the staff may have noticed that the child's manner has changed – perhaps from being lively and interested to being withdrawn – and discussing this with the parents elicits the information that something unknown lies ahead.

In the nursery, the staff can support the child and ease fears. Setting up a hospital corner and explaining what the equipment is used for can be a big help. Through 'being the doctor', the child can come to understand that the stethoscope or the X-ray machine, which appears terrifying, doesn't hurt. Even going to the dentist can be turned into a positive experience.

Listening to stories, e.g. 'Topsy and Tim go to the dentist' and studying the pictures can help the children to understand what will happen. Staff can talk about all aspects of their visits so that they are prepared in advance and lose the fear of the unknown. Other children might like to share their experiences too. The children should also know that stickers awarded by the doctors or dentists can be brought into the nursery and shown to the other children afterwards.

Imaginary fears

Children can have imaginary fears which upset them deeply. Often they know that they are not real and so they are reluctant to explain what they are, or they may not have the language to describe their worries.

Case study: Katie

Although Katie's parents assured the staff that she was toilet trained, at nursery wet pants happened most days, often more than once. This upset the parents, the child and the staff who began to worry about possible illnesses. Jane, a member of staff who had particular responsibility for Katie, had regularly offered to take her to the toilet, but this was met by crying and kicking. One day, however, Katie explained to Jane that she was afraid someone would be looking up at her as she sat down. Hand in hand, Jane showed her the pipework behind the toilet 'that couldn't let anyone's neck get round', then just in case Katie wasn't convinced they flushed the loo twice 'to flush him away' so that he could never come back again!

Communicating with parents, staff and students

Notice boards

The notice boards are a very useful means of communicating many different kinds of information. Many notices can be duplicated for staff and parents' boards while others are for display on either one or the other. The notices will attract interest if they are on crisp, coloured card and regularly changed so that the most important current information is posted.

The following information can be posted:

- Staff names, 'titles' and photos to ease communication;
- Holiday dates;
- Notices about outings;
- Invitations for parents to help and suggestions as to what they might like to do;
- Newsletters;
- Notices about head lice asking parents to check the whole family (leave this in place for two days when a specific case has been discovered or it loses its effectiveness);
- The year plan;
- Special topics which have arisen, e.g. 'making kites' or 'new babies';
- Children's names and times when they will be in the nursery.

Obviously the notices will change according to the activities currently being resourced and taught, any outings that are planned and any fund raising that is going on. The notice board also offers an opportunity to explain the learning that the children are experiencing.

Sample notices

For parents and staff notice boards:

Parents' notice board: Early Numeracy

Early Numeracy is supported throughout the nursery on a daily basis in the following ways.

Mathematical language

Balance, heavier, lighter – baking, dough, compare bears
full, empty, $^1/_2$ full, $^1/_2$ empty etc (water, sand)
longer, shorter, fatter, thinner etc (dough, bricks)
1 more, 2 more (measuring activities, counting activities)
next, first, last etc (turn taking, games, bikes etc)
2D + 3D shape (sides, corners, faces, edges)

Number

Counting, dice-dots or numbers, magnetic numbers, number posters, numbers at snack, singing games (counting up and down, books)

Shape 2D + 3D

2D + 3D shapes, posters, books, magnetic shapes, wooden blocks
Computer programmes, shaped paper/gluing items, dough cutters
Comparison of shapes (similiarities and differences)

Colour – global

Sorting, matching, grouping
Variety of resources, also matching cups to saucers etc.
Tidying, matching items to outline shapes in cupboards

Time

Days of week (today, yesterday, tomorrow)
Snack time, tidy up time, lunchtime, home time etc.
Sequence of events i.e. tidy is before story
Turn taking (next, last, etc.)
Egg timer and kitchen timer for turn taking or baking

Position

General conversation and instructions
i.e. put it *in* the box.
    can you go *through* the tunnel?

Problem solving

Construction, sand water etc.
What do you think will happen?
What can you make/do?

Parents' notice board: Early Literacy

Early Literacy is supported throughout the nursery on a daily basis in the following ways.

Story

Opportunity to discuss author, title, illustrator; To predict and recall events; To demonstrate left to right tracking. Traditional tales, modern stories, poetry, rhyme and alliteration. Story sacks. Books can be borrowed from the nursery library

Print in the environment

Children's names at coats, snack, gluing book, writing table. Snack menu. Baking picture/word books, children's telephone number books, shopping list book, alphabet posters (English and Arabic) magnetic letters, days of the week and weather cards, labelling/captioning. Computer use.

Sounds

Alphabet hanging (sorting), alphabet jigsaws (upper and lower case). Big book letters, sounds lotto, rhyming lotto game. Letter sounds lotto.

Writing

Letter formation sheets for parents
Paper, pens, pencils always available
Cards, envelopes when appropriate
Paint, chalk, sahara sand tray
Scribing for children's pictures, photo stories.

Talking

Staff take every opportunity to extend vocabulary and support children in their conversations.

Parents' notice board: Food in the Nursery

We aim to provide a healthy snack that is suitable for all the children including those with specific dietary and religious requirements. Some differences can be eased by shopping for a vegetarian option, e.g. vegetarian cheese. The foods purchased should clearly display the vegetarian logo.

Eggs – only free range eggs

Margarine – a good quality sunflower spread with the vegetarian logo (no 'savers brands')

Cheese – white, mild, vegetarian

No meat or nuts

Stock cubes – vegetarian only

Food colourings to be avoided (in case of allergies)

Fresh fruit and vegetables – daily provision of one essential

Milk and water are always available

Fruits: seedless grapes, oranges, apples, pears, melon, bananas etc.

Exotic fruits: kiwi fruit, star fruit, avocado pears, mango, pawpaw

Dried fruits: sultanas, pitted dates (staff always check that any dried fruit mixtures have no added colouring or sugar)

Vegetables: carrot stocks, baby tomatoes, sliced peppers, cucumber

Plain biscuits and crackers

Cereals

Porridge

Marmite (can be mixed with margarine or butter for easier spreading)

Yoghurt

Bread and rolls

Nursery Family Outing
Monday 25 June

The family outing this year is to North Berwick. North Berwick has many attractions – the beach, the harbour, a fantastic playground, trampolines, crazy golf, miles of grass, cafés and shops.

Just in case the weather is poor, we have booked a hall a short distance from the harbour. If it is nice, we could leave our picnics and coats here; if it pours we will shelter and play games with the children, although building sandcastles in the driving rain and gale force winds can be fun!

The buses leave school at 9am and we return at 3pm in time to meet older brothers and sisters.

The cost is £3.50 per seat. Infants under two are free – everyone else must have their own seat. Booking sheets are on the notice board. An adult must accompany each child. School age children are not allowed – they have to go to school!

Seats can be paid for on Wednesdays from 2 May until 13 June but please fill in your name as soon as you know you wish to go. The last day for payment is Tuesday 19 June.

K. McVitty (Nursery Teacher)

Figure 3.14 An example of a letter to parents about an outing. Individual letters home are backed up by a copy posted on the parents' notice board

Students on placement

(For both the staff and the parents' notice boards.)

Students

Over the course of the session, there are likely to be several students arriving in the nursery for their placements, i.e. the practical, hands-on part of their training. They may be school-leavers, mature students, nursery nurse students or teacher education students. They will be at different stages in their training and so have no/little/lots of experience of nursery age children and/or nursery education. The nursery teacher has the responsibility of overseeing their progress and tutors from the appropriate educational institutions will also visit.

Nursery nurse students – 2-year full-time college training, learning about children 0–5

Teacher education students – 4-year university training, learning about children 3–11

Postgraduate students from different university courses – 1-year PGCE university training, learning about children 3–11

The different training demands in each of these courses means that the nursery cannot take previous experience/expertise for granted – and even where it exists, the ethos, the expectations and the staff team differ from one context to the next. In many ways, this makes each placement 'a fresh start' for the students, with each one needing time to settle, to get to know the children and build relationships with them, and time to practise their observation skills – in other words time to acclimatise to each new, very complex environment. Most students will observe the children at first under the supervision of the nursery teacher, gradually building their interaction and teaching skills so that they become part of the nursery team.

Guidelines for students

This could be displayed on the staff notice board with a copy for each student's file.

Guidelines for Students

We enjoy having students in the nursery and hope that you learn a great deal in your time spent with us. It is important that you become part of the team as quickly as possible. We appreciate that there is a lot to learn so we are ready to answer any questions. Please read the staff notices and be clear about the information posted on the parents' notice board. Some information to help is listed below.

- Punctuality – staff begin at 8.30am which is when planning and setting up starts.
- If you are ill, please phone the school by 8.30am [telephone number here].
- Confidentiality – discussions about the children's progress are *confidential*. This is critically important for safety as well as professionalism. Please ensure that no child can be identified by any comment you make outside the nursery.
- Professionalism – be professional in your dealings with parents and staff at all times. Show the children that you respect them – learn their names quickly and smile as you greet them. Get down to their level so that you can listen to them carefully and try to respond in a way that encourages them to talk with you. Respect the children's work, e.g. handle their gluings carefully and be positive in all your interactions with them.

    If you suspect a child has a difficulty, share this immediately with the teacher in charge. Do not attempt to deal with it yourself as there may be circumstances which could make this inappropriate and even harmful.

    Keep talk to professional matters in working time.

- Responsibilities – check your particular responsibilities for the day in advance and make sure you ask for any help/clarification you need.
- Planning and paperwork – this needs to be shared with the experienced staff in time for any amendments to be made. Your file is a professional document and should be tidy as well as detailed! Change the name of the nursery and the children's names before it is handed in at college or university. (Check what each institution advises as this may differ from one to the other.)
- Children's guidelines:
    We are kind to each other and look after each other's work.
    Rough games are not allowed.
    We walk and work quietly in the nursery.
- Staff guidelines:
    Staff should not sit on the tables – crouch down or sit beside the children. Tables are for eating or working.
    Staff do not shout except in an emergency.
    Staff share any concerns with the teacher in charge. Any comment made by a child which could be seen as disclosure should be accepted without reaction, written down exactly as soon as possible and reported immediately to the teacher in charge. While the head teacher will decide whether or not to report it, no other member of staff should talk with the child about what was said.
- Parents' guidelines:
    When parents wish to consult with staff they should *always* come into the nursery rather than stand in the doorway with a buggy or pushchair. An open door can allow a child to slip out.
    Appointments can always be made in advance, usually for the end of the day. Parents must realise that, except in emergencies, they cannot just arrive and expect to spend time with the staff.
    Parents are encouraged to bring their children on time and to read the notices on the Parents' notice board.

Staff notices

This information should be for the staff notice board only – not accessible to parents.

- Children who require medication;
- Children who have allergies/dietary restrictions;
- Termly diary sheet;
- Useful contact telephone numbers (e.g. Children and Family Centre, health visitors, minibus firms, local farm);
- Year plan, monthly plan, lists of children's interests, daily organisational plan;
- In-service course provision.

Display area for parents

The display area can help parents understand the teaching that goes on in the nursery by showing the level of the input. Useful displays might be:

- A4 folders of favourite recipes. Some parents might like to try to bake or cook with their children at home. The children, having practised at nursery, can be 'in charge' so boosting their self-esteem. Repeating an activity also allows them to recall the planning that was needed as well as reinforcing their motor skills.
- Favourite songs and poems. Sometimes parents enjoy learning these too and sharing them with their children at home – the children's rendition alone may baffle them!
- Constructions/drawings/craft work and other items the children have made. It is important that every child knows that his or her work will be on display at some time.

Choose a plain cloth draped over cardboard boxes to provide plinths of different heights that will display the items to their best advantage.

Photographs and fund raising

Parents usually enjoy having pictures of their children engaged in a nursery activity. If these are mounted on card they can make a colourful display on the notice board and later they can be sold to the parents for 20p or so to defray expenses. The photograph will communicate to parents the kind of learning their children are engaged in.

At Christmas the children can decorate cheap wooden photo frames with items from the gluing table. After they are varnished they make lovely presents or they can be sold as presents for children and mums to give to Granny!

Fund raising is a continual activity in the nursery and can be problematic in areas of deprivation. Regardless of the type of area, it is preferable that parents who wish/are able to support the nursery should have something in return for their money, e.g. the photo frame described rather than just having a chance to win a raffle.

Raffles

A raffle where tickets are only sold in the nursery does not need a licence, but one is required for books of tickets that are sent home.

Other fund-raising ideas:

- A coffee morning where the parents contribute cakes and buns;
- A used toy sale (staff have to check that games are complete);
- A jumble sale;
- Lottery Bonus Ball (Saturdays).

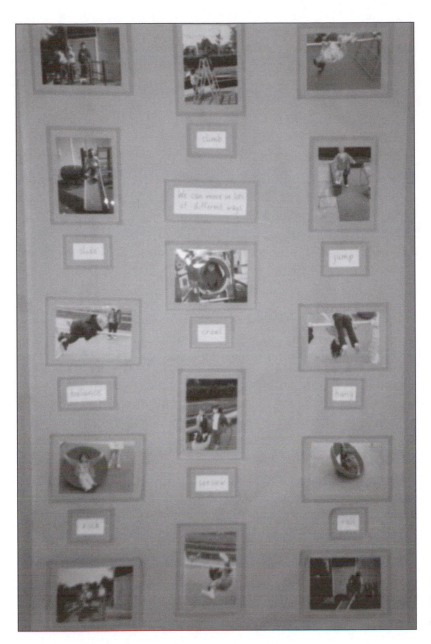

Photos of children working in the outdoor area – a display for parents

For the Lottery Bonus Ball game, the numbers 1–49 are sold for £1 each. The person who has the number corresponding to the Saturday night bonus ball wins £20 (assuming that more than 20 parents wish to participate otherwise this figure needs to be adjusted) – any surplus goes to the nursery funds to provide resources and treats for the children.

Sponsored obstacle courses and 'nursery rhyme marathons' are also good ways to raise funds. The latter needs a great deal of preparatory teaching but the parents can collect contributions from relatives and friends.

All of these suggestions need preparation and planning, so this time element has to be considered during planning meetings.

Planning outings

Any outing needs careful planning. Staff should visit the proposed location first to check out, e.g. child friendliness and suitability, learning potential, distance to and from the nursery and the possible means of transport. Some important questions that need to be answered are:

- Are three- and four-year-olds genuinely welcomed?
- Are the safety/security measures good, e.g. sound fencing in place?
- Is there a first-aid post?
- Are there toilets at different places?
- Is there somewhere to leave lunchboxes and coats?
- Is there somewhere under cover to eat?
- Is drinking water available?
- Is the distance between 'exhibits' suitable for three- and four-year-olds?
- Is there suitable shelter if it rains?
- How far is the car/bus park from the venue?
- Is a member of staff prepared to help with arrangements on the day?
- Is the total time (travelling there, the venue itself and the return time) suitable for the envisaged group of children, remembering that excitement may mean reduced sleep the night before?
- Are cancellation arrangements possible? This could mean a partial refund of costs in the event of unexpected events necessitating cancellation.

Once these initial checks have been made on the venue and the nursery staff have decided that the trip should go ahead, the following arrangements have to be put in place.

1. Inform parents early by letter and check permission slips are up to date. If not, send out updated slips. Put the prepared notice on parents' notice board and a duplicate in the staff room (there may be supply staff on duty who were not involved in the original preparation).
2. Work out the cost and organise the collection of money one week before the outing. Discuss with staff the problems of non-payment.
3. Decide on the number of children who should go – all the children or only the four-year-olds? This decision means considering the children, the level of help that parents can promise and the scale of the venue. Whether the children are always together as one whole group or whether the groups separate and meet again can influence the number of adults needed to supervise the children.

Some considerations are:

- Will all the children behave sensibly in a new environment? If any child is likely to become overexcited, needing constant one-to-one care, this would impact on the decision regarding numbers.
- The staff:pupil ratio for outings will be set by the local authority, but the nursery staff, who are familiar with the children in their care, may decide that more adults are required. Again this depends on the nature of the trip – a visit to a local nature reserve would be likely to require fewer adults than a visit to the zoo or the seaside. Some outings with four-year-olds could be accomplished with a ratio of one adult to four children, but most outings require a higher number of adults. One adult for every two children is the minimum if there are any roads to be crossed as this allows all hands to be securely held. It is best to err on the side of too many helpers. It is also a good idea to have back-up help available – if just one adult fails to turn up for any reason, the outing could have to be postponed leading to great disappointment all round.

Larger group outings

For these outings the nursery staff should organise groups, e.g. 1 member of staff: 4 helpers: 10 children.

- Mobile phones: in a larger outing where the groups may not be together all of the time, it is essential that each member of staff has a mobile phone and the contact numbers of the other groups.
- First-aid kits: each member of staff should carry a first-aid kit in case of emergencies. The telephone number and whereabouts of local hospitals should be checked in advance of the trip.
- Master lists: the staff notice board should have a master list of the adults and children in each group.
- Choosing and organising helpers: the selection process has to be handled carefully. Staff can assure all potential helpers that their names have been put on a list but for a myriad of reasons, e.g. a parent wanting to bring a baby along, not all are suitable helpers.

Note: No helper should be left alone with the children. There should always be a member of staff present in case police checks have not been completed. Different authorities have their own policies and these need to be checked before arrangements are made. Once adults have agreed and been selected to help, however, they should be sent/given a brief letter confirming their responsibilities.

```
Dear Mrs Smith,

Outing to Children's Farm on Tuesday, 6 June 10am—12.30pm

Thank you for agreeing to be one of our adult helpers on this
outing. The children benefit from outings like these and we
depend on adult helpers to make this possible. We hope you enjoy
the day. If you would like to note things which sparked interest
in the children or perhaps the things they said they liked best,
we shall follow these up in discussions with the children.

Yours sincerely,


M. Scott
(Nursery Teacher).
```

(See Fig. 3.14 above for an example of the letter that will have been sent in advance to all parents informing them of the planned outing.)

Transport arrangements

- Coaches must have seat belts fitted;
- Cars require a three-point belt and properly fitted booster cushions. The drivers/owners must have business insurance cover.
- It is important that local authority regulations are checked in advance of the visit.

Local outings

More casual trips can take place on foot in the local environment. One member of staff to two children is required so that hands can be safely grasped. If possible, arrange for the children to take photographs so they can recount their 'adventures' to the whole group at nursery afterwards.

Case study: outing to the canal

Debbie, a nursery nurse, explains:

> A canal was being constructed near our nursery and alongside many of the children's homes. Huge clearing equipment was in daily use. The staff decided that two boys who had shown particular interest in the construction should be given a disposable camera and be encouraged to make a record of an outing. Due to the dangers on a construction site, this was restricted to the public access paths, but when the workmen saw the children watching they came out to where a parked JCB was waiting and allowed them to sit inside to have their picture taken. The children were thrilled!

> The workmen told them about the canal – why it was being made, where the water was to come from and about the precautions they had to take when driving large machinery. Afterwards the children decided which photos they would like to take and snapped their most interesting scenes.

> Then they took their camera to the chemist who explained what would happen to their film. The next day they collected their photos and chose some to make into a special book which was laminated. The two boys then shared their adventure with the other children using their book as a visual aid! This was especially pleasing as previously one of the children had not had the confidence to speak out. Now he didn't want to sit down!

Susan, Danya, Rachel and Emma enjoyed their visit to the fire station

Case study: outing to the fire station

As an earlier request for children to visit the fire station had been refused, Fiona decided to walk two children past the station in the hope that some engines would be going in and out. Two girls had been enthusing about an old video (*Trumpton*) they had seen at home and they came into the nursery chanting the names of the firemen (Barney, Dibble etc.). They were obviously intrigued by the engine and the parts the firemen played, so a walk to the fire station was to be their local outing. Again the girls were given a disposable camera so that they could make their own record.

The station looked very quiet so Fiona rang the bell and the small group waited with some trepidation. It turned out that two firemen were happy to spend their break time showing the girls around. They were allowed to sit in an engine and watch how the doors were operated. They were delighted when the men in uniform posed for their photos! Like the boys, they followed up their visit by taking the film to be developed, collecting the photos and compiling their very own book. They then shared their experiences with the rest of the envious group!

The criteria covered by this outing were:

Emotional, personal and social development (EPSD) 1
Communication and language 5, 6, 7, 8, 10, 12
Knowledge and understanding 1, 5, 6, 7, 12
Physical development and movement 6
Creative and expressive development 1

4 Provision and organisation of resources

Organisation

The whole staff team must know where everything goes and be meticulous in keeping everything in order for safety reasons as well as immediate retrieval and good training! New items must be shown to all staff so that everyone knows what is available and how it works. This also means that the most appropriate resources can be made available to the children quickly so that their ideas can be developed and their enthusiasm sustained.

Setting up

Whenever possible, the children should be involved in resourcing the areas and in tidying away afterwards as these are valuable learning episodes. A member of staff could lift a box of construction equipment from the cupboard and then the children could learn to select the correct number, colour and size of pieces to resource an activity. Useful prompts can reinforce problem solving, e.g. 'How many do you think we will need?' The child counts out the pieces, helping basic counting or 'Which colour would look good beside the red ones?' 'Can you put the blue pieces on the shelf under the red ones?' This reinforces colour recognition within a problem-solving activity without asking closed questions, e.g. 'What colour is that?'

The concept of comparison of size can be brought in if appropriate, e.g. 'Are the green ones bigger or smaller than the red ones?' Displays of items ordered by size can provide a helpful visual aid for those children who have difficulty with the size concept.

More, e.g. 'How many more do we need to fill this shelf?' can be a very difficult concept to grasp, but some of the older children may try to estimate, then enjoy the challenge of working out the problem to see if they were correct.

Once the children have been involved in setting up and know where the various resources are located they can be helpers at tidy-up time too. This gives them a sense of responsibility and achievement and is good training in self-discipline. However, some cupboards must be protected with locks (for the storage of medicines, handbags, confidential reports or letters); the children must learn that only members of staff may open them. The storage hut for outdoor equipment is definitely out of bounds to children in case the equipment should topple over and cause an injury.

Resourcing the areas: building up resources

There are many colourful resources in catalogues to stimulate activity (see 'Catalogues', p. 110); however, it must be emphasised that resources need not be expensive ones bought from a catalogue – in fact these can sometimes limit the children's imaginative play. Most parents will recall their child's fascination with the cardboard box which housed their expensive toy and ignoring its contents! Children may use cardboard boxes as secret hiding places, rockets or stimuli for their own imaginative games while rolling pins for baking can be made from a broom handle cut into lengths with the rough edges sandpapered. A collection of different-sized plastic bottles can be used for the water tray; corks can be used for printing, for floating in the water, even be sliced up (by parents or staff) for use at the woodwork bench. Parents can be encouraged to collect a variety of junk items, or bring in bits and pieces they no longer need. This helps them to feel involved in contributing to their children's education and provides a topic for positive interaction with the staff.

Preserving resources, keeping a master copy, sorting strategies

Whenever possible, laminate pictures and posters so that they can be wiped clean easily and will last much longer. As the curriculum goes into action, staff will be involved in making resources to augment those already provided or for reinforcement or extension work. These are time consuming and involve much careful thought about design and layout as well as the level of challenge. While staff are anxious to get these into play as soon as possible, a master copy should always be filed in the staff base. Duplication can save time later on when the originals are worn! Even if the original is no longer entirely appropriate, amending it is easier than designing a new one from scratch.

Sorting the resources

If there is a set of similar jigsaws or other games, then colour coding the back of each piece and the box allows easy sorting. The children can put all the red bits in the red box – a simple idea that saves lots of time!

Cleaning the resources

Once children have finished with plastic toys or construction kits, these need to be thoroughly cleaned before being stored to make them available immediately the next time they are required. Immersing the items in a large plastic bucket of baby sterilising liquid and leaving them overnight does the trick. If this is done regularly and meticulously, then the end of term 'big clean' is made that much easier.

Storing the resources

A large plastic translucent set of boxes on shelves is ideal. It can hold a set of labelled boxes and also be used as a divider to make play areas 'private'. The children are more likely to store their resources carefully if the storage area is clearly marked. They have to learn that although resources such as cars and lorries can move to any area, they have to be returned to the correct place at tidying-up time.

List of resources for fine motor skills with safety recommendations

- Staplers: although these are very useful when children want to make their own cards or books they should only be used with adult supervision – children using them should never be left unattended.
- Scissors: provide left-handed scissors as well as right-handed ones and colour code for easy identification. The children will then be able to select the correct ones quickly without fuss! Children have to learn:
  a) the correct way to hold the scissors;

  b) the correct way to carry them;

  c) that they cannot take scissors away from the cutting table without staff supervision or permission. This depends on the children's experience and reliability.

- String/wool: keep a ball of string in a box with a hole in the lid to save tangles and waste. The children can estimate how much they need and cut it. This is both good training in being careful with resources and good midline practice, i.e. two hands working at the midline of the body doing different things. Staff can observe whether the children have developed hand dominance.

- Felt pens: these give good results (strong, pleasing colours) and need little pressure which suits small hands.

- Pencils: chunky triangular pencils are good aids to early writing. Ordinary pencils can have special grips – there are many kinds to suit different hands. The rubber triangular types help many children adopt the correct grip.

- Coloured pencils: some children find it difficult to apply enough pressure to get a satisfactory result. The pale colours are often disappointing for very young children.

- Wax crayons: these do not sharpen well and they break easily. With chunky crayons the children may have difficulty seeing what they are producing.

- Paper and coloured card: a variety of sizes, colours and thicknesses can be provided (but make sure there are no sharp edges to cut little hands).

- Rolls of paper: these allow children to estimate how much they will need for wrapping a parcel. Cooperation between two children is usually needed to hold the paper and cut at the same time.

- Large sheets of paper give practice in folding and wrapping, while smaller pieces in different shapes can suggest 'things to make'. Some children love cutting for its own sake, so different weights of card offer a satisfying challenge.

- Glue: PVA glue gives better results than paste which can be lumpy and does not spread easily. Good construction with boxes is virtually impossible with paste – if the boxes don't stick the children become disheartened and lose interest in the activity.

- Extras for gluing: parents are often happy to collect junk, e.g. sheets of coloured wrapping paper from Christmas or birthday parcels, corks and feathers, ribbons from bouquets of flowers, small make-up boxes – anything that is safe and can be made into something else.

- Sellotape and masking tape: these are expensive but sometimes necessary to allow the children to make the model they have visualised in their heads. They are tricky to handle so staff may need to help some children to achieve their goal. This also helps prevent waste.

- Sorting tray: the sorting tray holds a variety of bits and pieces. Small, coloured paper shapes or sequins can decorate a birthday card, pieces of macaroni can be threaded then painted for a necklace. Pieces of paper doily or lace can adorn the children's work to make it more attractive. These kinds of activities are very good for developing fine motor skills.

Audai uses the pincer grip to make his selection from the sorting tray

Food items as resources (e.g. pasta, rice, beans): supermarkets will often provide out-of-date food items for threading and painting or decorating. Note: less is more! A small number of items (regularly topped up) will encourage careful gluing – too wide a choice can lead to too much being stuck on, obscuring any design or deft handling of small individual pieces of material.

- Glitter: while the children find this attractive, using glitter must be supervised at all times. Getting glitter into an eye causes serious problems.
- Cardboard boxes/tubes/kitchen rolls: the tubes can be cut into different lengths, labelled 'cylinders' and size ordered allowing discussion of 'biggest', 'smallest' etc. The children learn to appreciate length and width if they order the tubes in sizes as they tidy away or use them as part of a construction. Lots of learning about size and shape can come from comparing and contrasting junk, e.g. finding similar boxes from a selection; finding out how Toblerone boxes fit together to make a different shape; discussing the difference between cube and cuboid shaped boxes; finding that cuboids can stack while cylinders can't!
- Egg boxes: these can be used whole, cut into single pieces as holders or used to make dragon's humps!
- Large boxes: resources for the nursery usually arrive in large cardboard boxes that can stimulate lots of games as they become houses, castles, trains or spaceships. Put them in a large space or out-of-doors and the children's imaginations will soon take over! Sometimes they can provide a shelter for a child who needs to be private for a time. Flaps become doors and string handles can be attached.
- Small boxes: all sizes and shapes of boxes are useful for imaginative work. Boxes should be sellotaped shut so they provide a firm base for stacking or gluing. They can be ordered by size on the gluing shelf and labelled CUBOIDS. *Safety note:* foil trays and plastic tubs (e.g. strawberry boxes) can be very sharp when they are cut so they are best avoided.

Seasonal supplies for the nature table

Pine cones; acorns; coloured leaves; holly; a small vase of flowers; a hyacinth bulb in a transparent pot to show the roots growing as well as the flower; twigs with buds that will open.

Computers and software

This is a popular choice area especially when a new program arrives. It can be difficult to check these out for suitability in advance but other nurseries can often advise (see 'Catalogues', p. 109). Most programs for very young children are operated by the mouse only. Ideally children should learn to control the mouse before the keyboard is introduced. Thereafter children who have got used to finding their own name will enjoy finding their own letters on the keyboard.

Using the keyboard

Children are usually fascinated by the keyboard and anxious to try to type their names but things can get difficult because the keys only display capital letters. Some nurseries buy sheets of lower-case letters to place over the keys, while others prefer that the children recognise the capitals and come to grasp that two symbols, e.g. E and e, mean the same thing. One way to help is to make name cards for computer use, e.g.

> **A U D A I**
> **A u d a i**

Taking turns at the computer

Children may be reluctant to move on! A large egg timer can be used to ensure that all those who are waiting can take a turn within a relatively short space of time. If a new program has created a lot of interest these children can fetch one of their names from the gluing table and make a list. Each child then scores his or her name out when the egg timer tells them that the turn is over.

The sand in the egg timer tells Mohammed that his turn is nearly over. Also note the display of the children's computing work

Staff should be aware of the possibility that the use of a computer can hinder developing social skills. If they suspect that some of the children play endlessly on their home computers and have noticed that their social skills and language are not used to the full, then perhaps their use of the nursery computer could be limited. The children could sit in twos – one using the computer, the other waiting and watching or offering advice – to help prevent isolation, but it is a danger which has to be recognised and averted.

Software

There is a greater choice of suitable software for PCs than Macintoshes (see 'Catalogues', p. 110).

Encouraging role play

Making costumes

Most children have wonderful imaginations and will quickly improvise resources to meet their needs, e.g. the doctor's stethoscope from the hospital resources worn around the waist becomes a dog's lead – or worn on the head it becomes a personal stereo! While children can create their own resources, a bank of dressing-up costumes can provide a starting point for ideas or extend games so that the children's interest is sustained.

Costumes can be ordered from catalogues, but staff or parents with just basic sewing skills can make many items cheaply. Charity shops are good places to find material – a confirmation dress can be bought and become a bride's dress for 'weddings' – or parents may have unused pieces of material at home. A request on the parents' notice board can let them know just how useful such a donation would be!

Dressing-up clothes will be worn over the children's regular clothes so they have to be roomy, especially around the armholes and waists. Using a long length of velcro for fastening will allow the garments to 'fit' lots of children.

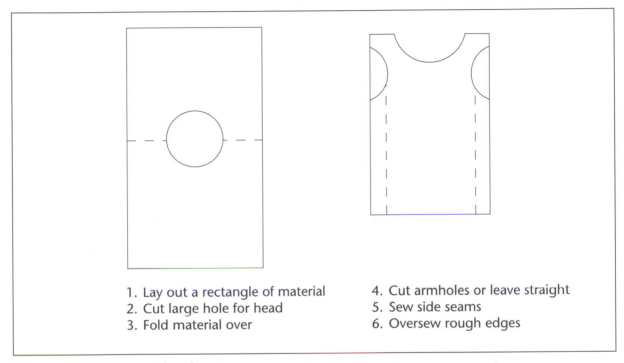

1. Lay out a rectangle of material
2. Cut large hole for head
3. Fold material over
4. Cut armholes or leave straight
5. Sew side seams
6. Oversew rough edges

Figure 4.1 Making a tabard

Kieran and Caitlin wear their tabards for the Nativity play

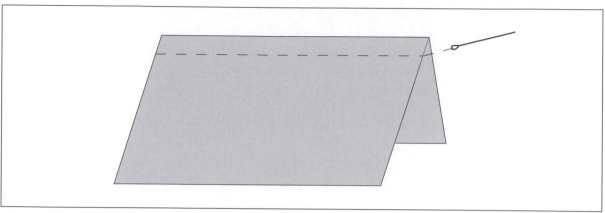

Figure 4.2 Making a tutu

Making a tutu for the dancing area

1. Fold a rectangle of net in half;
2. Sew a line of running stitches just below the fold. These should be large enough to allow the net to be drawn up;
3. Sew this into a waistband and attach some velcro for a fastener.

Longer skirts can be made in the same way. These stimulate role play.

Ethnic costumes

Parents will be able to advise staff where to buy appropriate materials and show them how to design costumes appropriately. They may be able to supply patterns, photos or actually help to make up the costumes for greater authenticity. Interest can be stimulated by home videos of families celebrating family events or festivals so the children can appreciate the dress in context.

This activity could be extended (i.e. family events and festivals) if parents are willing to come into the nursery to cook some food from their own culture. They might prefer to do this as a demonstration without involving the children to begin with, but as their confidence grows perhaps the children could help them to cook. This would be a natural extension once they get to know the children, the staff and the routine normally used in baking/cooking activities. The method of preparing the food and the ingredients to be used need to be discussed well in advance of the event (a deep fat fryer should not be used for obvious reasons and some children's dietary requirements might limit what they can eat, e.g. pork or nuts).

Puppets

Puppets – either bought or made – are ideal for imaginative play or to retell a story. Lovely, fluffy ready-made ones are available but some are so realistic, e.g. lions and tigers, that they could just suggest fighting in the jungle!! Sets of books, tapes and finger puppets are available for many traditional tales (see p. 110 for suppliers).

Children also enjoy and learn through making their own puppets. Small pieces of rolled cardboard can make finger puppets. Sock puppets often need some sewing – if an adult has to do this the children can still help design the puppet by selecting buttons or whatever is appropriate and determining what goes where.

Resources for the music corner

Children love to make music but buying instruments can be expensive. However, it is possible to make simple, percussion-type 'instruments' cheaply.

- 3 or 4 large bells from a pet shop (usually for cats' collars) can be strung on a circle of ribbon;
- Lengths of dowel can be cut and used as claves;
- At the gluing table the children can make simple shakers from yoghurt pots and dried haricot beans. Adults can cover the pots with clingfilm and fix the edges firmly so the beans can be seen but can't escape; alternatively the children can sellotape over cardboard, the adults checking that the container is secure;
- Large tins with plastic lids, e.g. catering size coffee tins, make acceptable 'drums';
- Empty tissue boxes with strong elastic bands stretched over the hole can simulate guitar strings and will make a 'pinging' noise (children should be supervised).

It is worth looking in the science section of catalogues as they often offer sets of chime bars or tuned bells at a more reasonable cost than those featured in the music section.

Small world

These are colourful, miniature items which stimulate play. The children can relate to the farm animals and trains readily as they are part of their own environment and can use the blocks and tunnels imaginatively to create scenes and events, e.g.

- doll's house with garden/playground toys
- cars and garage resources
- aeroplanes and airport resources
- village set
- train set

Many small world resources link with other areas of the nursery so the children learn to choose and select appropriately to complement the learning that is taking place in these other areas.

Resources for the house corner

Domestic play is always popular and so the house corner needs to be well resourced. Catalogue furniture is expensive but it is safe (i.e. it doesn't topple over or contain splinters). If cushions or seats or cot mattresses (for beds) are brought in from home, they must be made from fire-resistant materials – this has to be checked carefully to comply with safety regulations.

The house should belong to the children and adults should only enter when invited to do so! A three-section clothes horse with net curtains can give the children ownership by making the area seem private while still allowing staff to see what is going on. This is essential for making observations (see Ch. 6) and for safety. The children can make items for the house: their own pictures can decorate the walls; they can make a TV set or a remote control from boxes at the gluing table.

Minimum resources

- Cooker, pots and pans
- Sink or washing-up bowl
- Chairs, table, place mats, dishes and cutlery
- Bed and bedding, cupboard for storage, doll and cot

Telephones

If there are two telephones in the house corner the children can chat to one another. If old mobiles are used the batteries or the aerials should be removed. An old-fashioned dialling model helps precision (fine motor skills). Some children find it easier to carry on a conversation one step removed as it were – in this case, interaction skills are also encouraged.

House phone book

The children can be helped to make their own telephone directory using numbers appropriate to the age and stage of the child, e.g. Susan 12 or Jason 9801.

Scott and his phonebook

Children's phone books

The children can make their own phone book. Obviously the amount of support will depend on the age and ability of the individual children but there is a great deal of learning involved. This is also a more realistic and personal activity than having an adult full size directory.

The children find and cut out their own name from the alphabetical lists provided at the gluing table. They then choose 3 or 4 numbers from number cards (perhaps the younger ones using 0–3 and the most able using 0–9) and write these or have them scribed for them. A small cardboard booklet can then house their names and numbers (see photo of Scott and his phone book). A similar phone book can be made with 999 numbers, the local pizza place, the library or swimming pool, i.e. places the children might phone from home.

Children should be allowed to take resources from other areas into the house corner, especially if they add quality to the play, e.g. dressing-up clothes can help the characterisation in role play.

Similarly, house corner resources may be taken to other places, e.g. cups and saucers may be used for a picnic in the story corner, although a different set should be used for outside play.

There are four provisos, however:

1. The first is that these 'other items' should extend the play in some way – the children should not just accumulate items or carry things back and forward just for the sake of it. While there should be a genuine play reason this may not emerge until the play is underway, so adults have to observe closely to find the meaning in the activity rather than asking too early for explanations (see also Ch. 6, p. 97).
2. The second is that the items cannot be removed if that means that someone else's game is spoiled. The children should learn to ask rather than snatch!
3. Moving the resources should not result in the rest of the nursery being trashed.
4. The children have to realise in advance that they have to replace all the resources in their correct place. This helps both their organisation and sense of timing (the time needed to tidy will be in proportion to the number of items to be replaced).

Setting the table

Place mats showing settings can be made by the staff. These can be colour coordinated to match the teaset (to allow matching activities). If there are four cups and saucers, then four teaspoons are needed. If numbers are kept constant, i.e. always four forks, four plates etc., then the children know how many they have to find and replace in the cupboard at tidy-up time. This is a fun way to learn about one-to-one correspondence (see p. 61).

Tidying away

The shelves in the cupboard can have matching coloured stencils to show where each item goes; this helps colour recognition as well as organising skills.

Hannah tidies the pots. Note the stencils to show her where to place them

Additional interchangeable resources

These can be used as play develops or to suit the available space:

- If linoleum covers the floor in the house corner, then dough can be 'baked at home' so pastry cutters and small rolling pins are required.
- Dolls' furniture, e.g. a high chair, cot, buggy. A selection of dolls' clothes with different fastenings. Baby bath and towel.
- A variety of dishcloths and towels, small brushes for the dishes and a large one for sweeping the floor.
- Some hardboard books so that the children can 'read' to the dolls or each other.

Shopping

'Going to the shops' often develops as a way of resourcing the house corner supplies. The children discuss what is needed and with the teacher's help they compile a list. These items can be imaginary, collected from small world resources or bought by a real trip to the shops. This can involve recalling what was required, paying for the items and learning to pack them (eggs and cakes on top) ready to carry back to the nursery. To encourage this extension, a shopping list, pencils and pens should be available in the house corner.

Many resources can spark imaginative play. Children should learn to share, to take turns and to respect the resources – all of these experiences help them cope with the activities which they will need to learn at all the different stages of their education.

5 Enhancing early learning and practical ideas for activities

Opportunities for early literacy

This is supported throughout the nursery on a daily basis in the following ways.

Name recognition

If the children's names are placed beside their coat pegs, they see them immediately they come into nursery. This makes them feel welcome and reassures them that they belong. Being able to recognise their names also gives the children a feeling of confidence and achievement. Knowing where to hang their coat and being able to do it is also the first basic piece of planning/ organisation the children have to learn! Many nurseries place a picture alongside each child's name and this same picture is repeated at snack and in other places where name identification is important.

An alternative strategy which encourages the children to recognise their name without relying on a picture is to print the names on different colours of card for each child. The same colour is then used for name cards at snack. It is important that the pieces of card are the same length otherwise the child might recognise 'the long one' rather than the name itself!

Names always appear:

- At snack, when the children have to find their name and put it in a special place to show that they have had their turn. The children have to search for their own colour and then study the card to see which is theirs (there could be several cards of each colour). Staff are needed to support this early search, perhaps helping the children to recognise the first letter of their name (which should be handwritten). If two children have the same name, these should be written on different coloured card to differentiate.

- At the writing table the colour coding can be removed so that all the children's name cards are the same colour. This immediately identifies those children who have still to recognise their names, so staff can move in to support them. Setting up for the two sessions is simplified by using one colour of card for the morning children and another for the afternoon group.

  Gradually some of the children will want to write their own names and this is always encouraged. At the start of emergent writing, they may only produce a scribble, but this attempt is important and should always be respected. Sometimes staff can come to identify the owners of individual scribbles. Time should be spent writing with the children, but as this is not always possible at the 'right time', sheets of names have to be available.

- At each activity area when the children stick their name onto their picture/gluing to take home.

To encourage both name recognition and cutting skills an A4 folder with sheets of (computer-generated) names should be provided. These can be arranged in alphabetical order separated by layers of coloured card.

Name recognition is part of the routine at snack

If the names of the three-year-olds are cut into strips, the children have to make only one cut. However, the preschoolers should have a whole page so that they are encouraged to cut round all four sides of their name in order to give practice in controlling scissors and being accurate. Once the children have learned to cope with this they will not need to interrupt the teacher or nursery nurse, who might be otherwise involved elsewhere.

Names should be ready for immediate access at the writing and the gluing tables – in fact any area where the children can name their work instils the habit of so doing. This practice is continued in primary classrooms so it is a useful habit. In addition, names help the staff to identify the correct piece of work for the children to take home.

Story time

At story time the children learn about the author, the illustrator and the characters in the story as well as following the story line itself. Staff should remember, however, that the story is of prime importance – if the children are restless, any delay in reading it may result in a loss of attention. The children also learn to predict through interjections such as 'What do you think will happen next?', or 'How do you think (character) will feel now?' and so realise the effect of cliffhangers. They also enjoy relating events in the story to their own experiences, e.g. 'Has anybody been to the seaside like Jack in the story?'

Stories that rhyme are very popular as the children can join in, or, in stories such as *The Little Red Hen*, the children can wait for the punchline and call it out at the correct time. Sometimes they enjoy drawing the characters from their favourite story.

Figure 5.1 Dionne has drawn one of the characters from her favourite story, *The Three Little Pigs*

Story groups

If there is a difference in the children's ability to sit, listen and follow the meaning/structure/ sequence of a story, then it can be helpful to divide the children into groups so that the content of the story is matched more closely to their ability to listen/discuss. The less able children benefit by being in a group of five or less so that they can interact more easily. Some children need chairs or bean bags to support them and help them listen. The children's level of participation should be observed and recorded so that they have the chance to move between groups if their interest/ability changes.

If staff rotate round the groups each week they can note the progress of all the children.

Tracking

As the children listen to the stories the teacher can indicate the way words are read, e.g. in English from left to right, so that the children can follow the sequence of words as they are heard. This establishes the pattern in their minds and lets them practise early tracking skills. Dual language books demonstrate to the children that different languages require other directions for tracking symbols and sounds.

Other genres

The children should have opportunities to listen to traditional tales, modern stories, poetry, and learn about rhyme and alliteration. Action songs are fun, they develop listening skills and if they involve touching body parts (e.g. 'Heads, Shoulders, Knees and Toes') they help body awareness too. They also engender a sense of working together and provide an opportunity for staff to observe rhythmical awareness and confidence, e.g. whether a child is willing to volunteer to go into the centre of the circle as in 'Sandy Girl'.

Learning to listen

Although the stories and poems will be short and eventful so that they hold the children's interest, not every child can listen, perhaps because they don't yet have the attention span needed to help them concentrate. Listening to rhyming words and having fun suggesting other words, e.g. 'big', 'pig', 'dig' is a helpful activity for the four-year-olds. They also enjoy making up silly rhymes to go with their names, e.g. Alanna Banana.

A basic listening centre can be set up with staff overseeing the children in the early stages. Story tapes, puppets and books are complementary stimulating resources.

Sounds

Sounds Lotto games are cassettes of everyday sounds with pictures to match encouraging careful listening. In Photo Sound Lotto (see 'Catalogues', p. 110) cassettes of sounds, e.g. animals, are provided along with pictures to match each tape which are very useful as an aid in developing listening skills.

Story corner

A selection of books of different levels of difficulty should always be available for the children to browse and select (see 'Books for preschool children', p. 111). Stories, poetry, information books, children's cookery books, simple origami, simple craft books, traditional tales, pop-up books, counting books, dual language books – the variety is immense.

Corbinn is engrossed in his story book

Josh is adding his footprints to this ▶ group picture

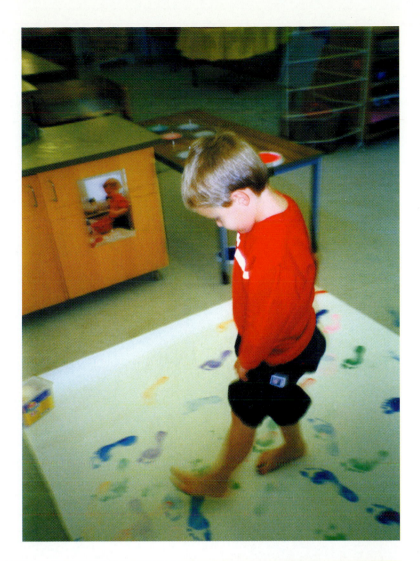

▼ Brandon chooses animals for the zoo he has built with blocks

◀ Brandon investigates how the water pump works

▼ The children explore the properties of snow

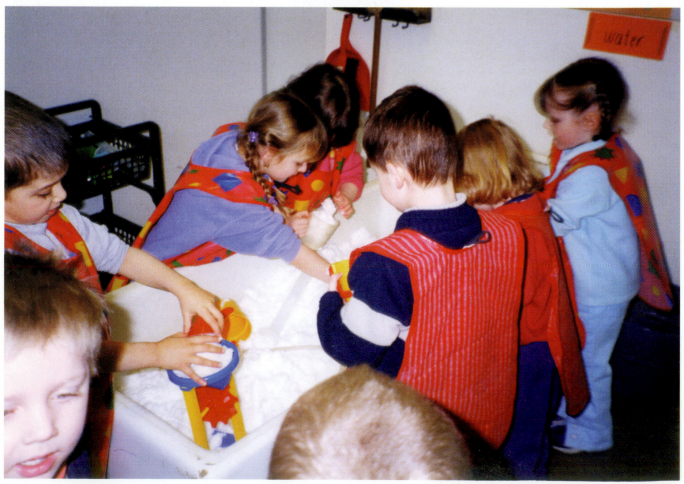

Audai finds the clay differs from the ▶
usual dough

▼ Shannon is engrossed in her
computer program

◄ Joel is listening to the story of the three little pigs on tape and using props to act out the story

▼ Hannah and Chloe celebrate the Chinese New Year

The lending library

A selection of a range of books can be built into a lending library:

- Longer and shorter stories (fiction)
- Traditional tales
- Dual language books
- Children's cookery books.
- Children's art and craft books
- Non-fiction books

A parent may be willing to act as librarian. A file should contain numbered list of the books with a corresponding number placed inside the book – if a parent forgets the title of number 12 it can be found easily! A special book to record 'borrowing' should include both the child's name and the date the book was taken home as well as the book number.

Story sacks

These can either be made or purchased commercially. They are expensive to buy so some organisation is needed before they are taken home.

The sack will contain appropriate toys, listening tapes, videos, puppets or a game to support the book, i.e. whatever resources are needed to make the story come alive. A 'gardening' story sack, for example, might contain seeds and compost, while a 'baking' story sack could include a rolling pin and cutters.

To keep a check on the contents, set out the contents of each sack on a table and take a photograph. One copy goes in the story sack so that when it is time to return it, the parents can check the contents against the photo. The other copy is filed in the nursery. This also serves as a check on what needs to be replenished, e.g. the compost is likely to need renewing frequently.

Early writing

The writing table

Josh is using his name card to help him name his work

It is important for children to have a table and chairs of the correct height so that they can sit in a balanced position to do their 'writing'. Feet should be supported on the floor as dangling legs don't provide stability – especially if they sway back and forward.

Resources

- Felt pens, pencils
- Paper clips, luggage labels, envelopes
- A sheet of stamps (1p), treasury tags
- Hole punches, staplers (only with adult supervision)

Triangular grips

Thick triangular-shaped pencils or pencils with triangular grips help children to use the correct tripod grip as they write. A whole variety of alternatives are available for children who do not find the basic rubber ones suit their hands. Children have to learn that these should stay at the writing table, not be taken into the house corner or used to decorate the walls!

Paper, envelopes and stamps

Sheets of paper of different sizes need to be provided for writing 'letters'. Several pieces can be stapled together to make shopping lists or policemen's notebooks.

Cheap envelopes make the activity real and fine motor skill practice is provided by folding the paper to the size that will fit into the envelope. The children can then 'write the address' and if a sheet of 1p stamps is available then the children can place them correctly and post the letter in a home-made postbox. Staff can slip the letters to mums at going home time so that they can appear on the mat at home.

Some children will wish to make their own books. Perhaps a nursery theme with the accompanying illustrated books has encouraged them to write and draw to make their own book.

Captioning children's work

When children's work goes on display it should be carefully mounted so that the children realise it has been valued and treated with care. It should also be captioned. The children can discuss their work with the staff, perhaps explaining their choice of colours, e.g. 'that purple bit's a deep pond not nice to swim in' or what the person in their picture is doing/seeing/even thinking, e.g. 'Mummy is a bit cross because she has to work in the garden!' Such interactions can lead to the child choosing a caption and being anxious to read it. This also gives the children the opportunity to watch someone write. Involving the children in this stage is much more productive than the child seeing the final product on the wall, the staff having determined what they think the picture is about and deciding on a (possibly wrong) caption.

Captions should be handwritten (except for computer work) because it is far more difficult to write a letter (think of the fine motor control needed to write 'a') than simply to press a key on the computer. Children watching staff to write are also helped to develop an interest in writing through being an 'apprentice.'

Opportunities for children to talk

It is important that children are encouraged to talk – to their friends, to recount an experience to a group and even to the whole nursery. Listening carefully and praising the children for their input gives them confidence in expressing their views – most will appreciate a clap from their 'audience' to say well done.

Staff interaction with children

Young children are still acquiring vocabulary and grammatical structures. 'I goed to bed' is the kind of phraseology that will pass! Staff have to help the children understand by substituting other words if their first input has not been understood and not be misled into believing that the children are being inattentive.

Jill, a nursery teacher, explains: 'I was fastening Malek's coat and wanted him to see how to do it. I said "Watch." He didn't. But as soon as I said "Look" he did!'

Questioning

This is a skill that needs a great deal of practice. Staff should try to visualise the kind of response they are expecting to get and if this is likely to be a one-word response, they should change their approach. For example:

Question: 'What colour are your shoes?'
Answer: 'Red!'

Try substituting a statement:

Statement: 'When I was a little girl my favourite shoes were just like yours. I wore them to parties.'
Answer: 'My mum always gets me red shoes because they are shiny and I can see my face in the toes. I had a party too but I didn't wear these shoes. We all had to take our slippers – that was very funny because Ann had giant ones...'

Success in extending children's talk very often depends on the type of input made by the staff.

Creativity and conversations

Young children are usually very satisfied with the art work they produce and are keen for their work to be viewed and praised. It is important to encourage this attitude, so staff have to be careful not to impose adult standards and make comments such as 'What's that supposed to be!' which are hardly likely to encourage the child to continue. Very often it can be difficult to discern what a painting is, so encouraging noises 'ooh' or phrases such as 'tell me all about this lively painting' or 'you have really worked hard to use all these colours' are more productive than making statements, e.g. 'I like your dog' which can be met by an incredulous stare – not surprising when the child has painted a cow in a field!

Creativity and expressiveness across the nursery

In every area in the nursery, the children's creativity is being encouraged. From role play in the house corner to art and craft and solving puzzles, the children are expressing their preferences and being given support to enhance these skills. Examples are given in the many activities later in the chapter.

Counting at snack

Opportunities for early numeracy/mathematics

Opportunities for early numeracy/mathematics are supported on a daily basis throughout the nursery in the following ways.

Recognition of number

The children count the numbers of children at snack (four spaces together) to see if there is a free place as well as the number of items they can have, e.g. 1 cracker, 1 piece of cheese, 2 pieces of mandarin orange etc. If the numbers are displayed prominently, the children gradually come to understand what each symbol represents.

Dice

Using extra large dice means the children have space to point to each dot as they count. Dice with colours or numerals are also available for variety and progress, but regular dice can be adapted by applying sticky labels.

Singing games

These can help counting too. 'Five current buns in a Baker's Shop' can be supported by pictures of individually numbered buns so the children can act out the song. 'Ten fat sausages, sizzling in a Pan', 'Ten in the Bed', and 'Five little speckled Frogs' are other examples.

Number posters

These should have large numbers and pictures to show that, e.g. 'The doll needs 1 vest, 2 socks, 1 coat.'

This was inspired by the computer program *Milly's Maths House*

Shape recognition: properties of shapes

The children should learn to recognise 2D shapes, e.g. squares, rectangles, triangles (discuss the number of sides/corners and show the difference between the long sides and the short ones) and circles.

Discuss the difference between the faces and the edges of 3D shapes, e.g. cones, spheres, cubes, cuboids, cylinders etc.

Comparing and contrasting shapes and sizes.

Children can use sorting trays plus a variety of items e.g. fruits to sort according to one of their properties, e.g. their size, colour or shape. Many resources for this are available in catalogues (see Appendix).

Colour recognition

Sorting, matching and grouping

Setting the table in the house corner (one-to-one correspondence of plates, cups etc.) involves both counting and matching as well as some aesthetics, e.g. choosing colours which go together, making the table neat, adding flowers etc. Tidying resources can involve matching the items to the outline shapes in the cupboards.

Chloë has set the table and invited Dionne and Shannon to tea

Time and routine

Children learn:

- the sequence of events, e.g. snack time comes before story time;
- that tidy-up time comes before going-home time;
- who is next (to have a turn);
- the meaning of soon and later;
- the days of the week and their order;
- about today, tomorrow and yesterday.

Kiera and Arran arrange the days of the week in the correct order

Timers

Egg and kitchen timers are useful resources to indicate times for changeovers (e.g. it's your turn when the sand has run through), or baking activities (we take the cakes out of the oven when the big timer is empty).

Mathematical language

General instructions can stress the 'position' words in many activities, e.g.:

- put the clay IN the box;
- put the apron ON the peg;
- put the basin UNDERNEATH the tap;
- climb THROUGH the tunnel;
- jump OVER the rope etc.

When working with dough, children can make the 'sausage':

- LONGER;
- THINNER;
- FATTER;
- SHORTER.

Playing with bricks can teach the children about:

- stacking one HIGHER;
- putting another brick BESIDE;
- putting the BIGGEST one UNDERNEATH.

The children can learn to make comparisons:

- Jon's castle is BIGGER/WIDER/HIGHER;
- The giant's boots are much BIGGER than Tom's.

Weighing

Using a two-pan balance demonstrates to the children the effects of being heavier or lighter. They learn how to estimate amounts which will make the pans balance and difficult concepts such as 'more' or 'less' may be introduced.

Problem solving

All the areas have this potential:

- Can you make…?
- Where can we put…?
- What can you do to…?
- Does that fit…?
- How will you…?

Early physical development and movement

The development of gross motor skills

In the nursery, the children must be given opportunities to develop their basic movement patterns, i.e. crawling, walking, sitting and standing, standing and sitting still, running, hopping and jumping. Some children will manage the combined patterns of running and jumping – even jumping from a height and moving straight into a forward roll – while others will be reluctant even to try to climb. Large apparatus needs to be carefully chosen to give the correct level of challenge; staff supervision is essential at all times because not all children have a realistic expectation of their own competence.

Regardless of whether the large apparatus is positioned indoors or outoors, its stability must be checked before being used by any child. This should be the responsibility of one staff member each morning and between each changeover of children. It is also important that there is a clear pathway for children to reach the apparatus and climb down from it without any other child obstructing either the approach or landing paths. Large landing mats are essential and should be placed anywhere where the possibility exists of a child falling from a height. It is possible to use large apparatus indoors in the winter months during inclement weather.

Charease loves to practise monkey climbing on the supported bar

The outdoor play area/safety issues

Safety is paramount all the time but particularly when the children are playing on large apparatus and there is a real possibility of a child falling. An outdoor, soft play area is ideal/essential if landings are to be safe. This can be costly (approx. £2,500 for a medium area) but the material does absorb falls; it also dries quickly so it can be used when other parts are still wet. It might be worthwhile applying for Lottery funding as it would be difficult to raise this amount by fund-raising activities. Each local authority has its own rules about surfaces within play areas which should be checked and adhered to.

The selection of outdoor apparatus must provide a range of challenges so that even the most timid children can try something — even if it's just stepping onto the broad side of a bench. Gradually, with encouragement, successes will result in a more confident approach. Staff should offer some support at first, e.g. 'Would you like me to hold your hand for this first time?' without taking the full weight of the child. If there is a likelihood that the child will get stuck and need lifting down, staff should suggest an alternative piece of apparatus until the child becomes more proficient. Subtle suggestions such as, 'Look at Jason crawling through the tunnel — I'm sure you could do that' is more positive than commenting, 'That's too hard, try this...!'

Resources

- Tunnels for crawling through — these should be clear plastic to allow the staff to see the children's crawling actions (very important for the development of coordination and spatial awareness) and so the children can see where they are going. Crawling is one of the most important actions for developing coordination and balance. Some children may never have crawled before and they should be helped to do so. If this proves to be particularly difficult, staff should carefully note this in their observations and if after several weeks there is no progress, try to get specialist help as it may be an indicator of a specific learning difficulty.
- A supported bar for climbing along or rolling around (the grip should be demonstrated, i.e. fingers should point back so that the large part of the hand controls the weight of the body when rolling over). Some children manage perfectly well using a fingers-forward grip, but (particularly for heavier children) having their fingers back is better as the body weight can be held back so that the feet can be pulled in to land near the bar.
- A climbing frame — ideally with a low and a high platform (to vary the climbing challenge). A chute may be attached to one of the bars so the children can slide down to land on a mat. The climbing action is a vertical crawling action with the added challenge of leaving the ground.
- Ladders for climbing — different slopes attached to rungs of different heights on the climbing frame.
- Chutes to allow sliding and learning to control the speed of an action.
- Spinning top. This very popular piece of apparatus (available from the Rompa catalogue, see p. 110) is excellent for developing awareness of the back; the children have to make strong use of their backs in order to make the top spin and they can alter their position to make it change direction. Sometimes more confident children can cooperate to make the top spin but this is not necessary.
- A range of different-sized bikes means that children of all heights and sizes can all be catered for. One-seater, two-seater trailer and trundle (no wheels) bikes all lend themselves to different balancing challenges and some require cooperative play. *Note:* bikes should never be allowed near the large apparatus. Apart from the contact danger, the movement could distract children who need to concentrate on their climbing or balancing skills and cause accidents.

Shannon helps Josh to spin the top

Josh, Arran and Dionne enjoy cycling in the garden

- Small apparatus, e.g. balls of all shapes and sizes, small bats, shuttlecocks, skittles and hoops. A range of small apparatus helps manipulative skills which involve hand–eye coordination, timing and rhythmic ability. Aiming skills can be developed by suspending empty, clean milk cartons on strings and encouraging the children to hit them using small bats. If the cartons swing back and hit the children they don't hurt. Alternatively, hoops can be suspended from a clothes line to see if the children can pass the ball to one another through the hoop. Following the path of a ball (tracking) can be a difficult skill for some children, so they should begin by sitting opposite a partner with their legs open and rolling the ball to one another. Once they wish to progress, encourage them to try a bounce pass first so they can see the ball and their hands all of the time. Staff can help the children to appreciate the rhythm by saying, 'bounce, catch – bounce catch' at the appropriate speed.

Ideas for practical activities

Making and using dough

Dough will keep for a week if stored in a sealed tub.

Resources

- **Day 1:** pot, whisk, jug, mug, 1 tablespoon, 1 teaspoon. Plain flour, salt, oil, cream of tartar. Aprons! Shaker of flour in case the dough is too soft for rolling.
- **Day 2:** rolling pins, pastry cutters of different shapes, pizza cutters.
- **Day 3:** coloured straws cut into lengths to make candles for the 'birthday cake'. Large buttons to make imprints.

Day 1

Activity	Teaching points
Measure 2 mugs of flour and tip into pot	Count spoonfuls of flour into mug. Estimate how many more need to fill it. Discuss half full, nearly full
Add 2 mugs of water (one child can pour while another mixes)	
Add 1 mug of salt	Talk about the differences between the flour (light, fluffy) and the salt (smooth, runny). Why add salt? (To keep fresh)
One child holds the tablespoon over the pot while the teacher pours the oil	Talk about the colour of the oil
Child adds 1 teaspoon of cream of tartar	Talk about the size of the teaspoon and tablespoon
Child whisks the mixture (the mixture will be lumpy then runny)	Stop, look to see the change in texture
The teacher then cooks the dough on the cooker top	Ask the children 'What do you think will happen?'
Children handle the warm dough, lengthwise to make snakes of various lengths, then top rolling to make it into different-sized balls	The soft dough is ideal for children who find difficulty applying pressure when rolling
Dividing the ball of dough into sections with plastic knives	Language development: big, small, long, short, fat, thin, round etc. Make patterns with buttons

Day 2

Activity	Teaching points
The dough will be firmer now, allowing the children to cut out shapes	Talk about cutter shapes and sizes; pressing firmly, lifting gently. Count the number of biscuits

Day 3

A group of children might decide to make one large 'birthday cake', adding 'candles' (short pieces of straws) for a toy in the nursery. They might suggest the toy's age and so decide on the number of candles they would need – or they might decide to prepare a party for some of the other toys in the nursery.

Possible developments

- Making party invitations or birthday cards for the toys; discussing what they would like to have at the party; what games the toys would like to play; what they would like to have for a birthday present. It's important to stress that everyone is invited!
- Talking about the temperature of the dough and the effect this has on the texture and what can be done with it. Changing colour should also be discussed. Cake colour might be added to make decorative shapes for the birthday cake but much of the learning can take place without colour being added at all (as that is not part of the basic process of mixing the ingredients).
- This can be a useful preparation for real baking.

Dough or clay

Clay should be offered every so often so that comparisons between it and dough can be observed. Clay is always cold and water sometimes needs to be added to keep it moist. Adding water to dough should be discouraged as it spoils the consistency for rolling and cutting.

Clay is firmer than dough, i.e. it is less malleable for small hands. Some children won't be able to apply the pressure to use cutters with clay, but items can be air-dried and painted so that the children have something to take home. Aprons must be worn.

Dough will keep moist in an airtight tin. Clay needs to be wrapped in damp paper towels then put in a tin or it becomes hard quickly. Scrapers are needed to clean the tables if clay is chosen. Linoleum flooring is best.

The sand tray – dry and wet sand

Dry (preferably silver) sand needs a deep tray to prevent it flying up into the children's eyes. It behaves like water, so similarities in pouring from jugs and over wheels can be pointed out.

For the wet sand tray the children can pour in some water to make rivers and have fun floating boats under adult supervision – otherwise the sand will become flooded by over-enthusiastic pourers!

The children can compare the textures and describe how each kind of sand could be used.

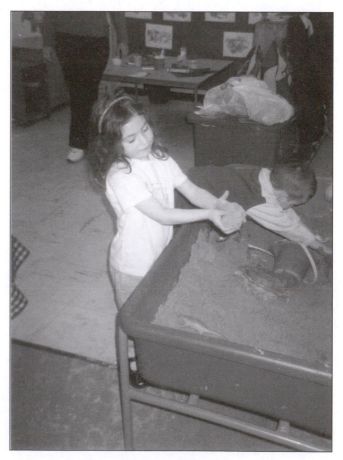

Shannon makes a sphere at the sand tray

Resources

- Dry sand: jugs; sand wheels; trowels; funnels of different sizes; cartons to fill; spoons from baby milk; sieves; shells in summer (these need constant checking for sharp edges).
- Wet sand: buckets and spades of all sizes to make castles or sand pies; moulds to fill with sand and then smooth off the surface; ice cream tubs and baby milk spoons (provide materials at the gluing table to make flags for the castle turrets).
- Toy diggers to make roads; plastic cars to run on them; traffic signs; toy houses and trees to make a village.
- Stones to shore up the sand, e.g. to make caves and so to stimulate imaginary work. Stones with patterns can lead to discussions about the different coloured layers and how they are made; they can also be used to make patterns or decorate sandcastles etc. (some can be painted).
- Empty whisky bottle tubes are firm and so make excellent tunnels.

Cooperative play

Children can build a village together. If some children don't seem to have any ideas and begin to lose interest, try placing a toy, e.g. a police car or an ambulance, in the sand to rekindle enthusiasm by sparking off ideas for developing the theme. This leaves the children with the ownership of the idea rather than having been given instructions. Use plastic rather than metal cars (they clog up less).

Vocabulary

Pouring, patting, heavy; light, full, empty; nearly full/nearly empty, wet, damp, dry. Estimating practice, e.g. how many scoops will fill the pail?

The water tray

Resources

- Jugs for pouring.
- Clear tubes for siphoning (for hygiene reasons children should not blow down tubes).
- Bottles to fill (narrow necks and wide necks).
- Ice cube trays.
- Eye dropper for adding colour. Water should only be coloured (using cake colour) if there is a reason for so doing, e.g. to show how colour from an eye dropper spreads. Ice can also be coloured to let the children see the effect of it melting and the colour spreading. Colour also makes observation of the movement of water in the tubes and syphons easier.
- Water toys with turning wheels.
- Funnels.
- Buckets with holes (to observe the shower effect as the water comes through).
- Jars and buckets of different shapes but the same capacity can help the children's understanding of conservation of volume. Holding a full bucket also needs concentration, strength and a steady hand so some children will need support.
- Boats, fishing games, water creatures, corks – objects that float and objects that sink.

(*Note:* creatures that live in fresh water, e.g. frogs, and those that live in salt water, e.g. sharks, should not be put in the same tank at the same time!)

- A large sieve or colander to drain the toys at tidy-up time.

Dionne and Dylan
learn about levels

Skills

- Pouring with control;
- Estimating volume;
- Learning about levels, reading levels;
- Midline practice – pouring with one hand and holding the receptacle with the other;
- Learning about temperature – the effects of adding 'more hot' or snow or ice;
- Cooperating in twos or threes.

Vocabulary

Ice: solid, freezing, crackly, transparent, melting, shrinking, disappearing. Colour: spreading, mixing, getting fainter, disappearing.

Winter theme

The children can make a snowman together (cooperative play), and place and count his buttons. They can also bring in snow from outside and completely fill the water tray to show them the effect of the warm room on the snow. This could link with *The Snowman* story and/or music to allow the children 'to dance like a snowman with large gallumphing steps then the sun comes so that they melt down slowly into a pool of water. At night time it's freezing again, so the snowman rises up, looks around, catches some snowflakes to eat and begins to dance again.'

Skills

Listening to music and following simple instructions. Simple role play, i.e. being a snowman who freezes and melts and freezes again.

Vocabulary

Floating, sinking, capsizing; refloating; bobbing up. Types of boats: barges, ferries, battleships, aircraft carriers, yachts, pedal boats. Water: clear, muddy.

Linked activity

Sailing 'boats' and discussing sinking and floating. Using plastic boats, cups, clothes pegs and plastic toy cars, the children experiment to find which items float and which sink and discuss why this should happen. The teacher could demonstrate prodding a boat, trying to make it sink, and the children could observe the way the boat keeps afloat despite the turbulence of the water. Adding small blocks to demonstrate how cargo is carried also provides new learning. The children can count how many blocks were carried before the boat toppled over or sank.

The children can fold paper to make paper boats and find if they float. Perhaps the older children would like to see pictures of decorated barges and this might encourage them to paint their own boats.

Making a junk robot

While this provides much fun it does need adult supervision and sellotape – or even stronger parcel tape to fix the pieces together and to find ways of stabilising the growing robot.

The activity is good for promoting body awareness through naming the different body parts. The less usual ones, e.g. ankles, elbows, heels, shoulders and backs can be stressed. It also helps the development of the imagination as the children give their robot a name, decide where he came from, where in the nursery he would like to live, when his birthday is and what stories he might enjoy. They might like to give him a scarf or paint his shoes. An interesting discussion could result from asking the children, 'What will our robot be able to do?'

The key learning is mathematical and perceptual as the children debate the suitability of shapes for different body parts, e.g. choosing shorter cuboids for the forearms, longer, stronger ones for the legs and two of similar size for the feet and hands. There should be a pool of different-sized cartons so that the children can select and reject. Perhaps they could build both a full-sized robot and a baby one to allow comparison of sizes and more mathematical language to be used, e.g. bigger, shorter, thinner, stronger etc.

Making gluck

This is a messy activity but one which is excellent for helping children to understand textures and the changing properties of objects. Aprons are essential.

Let children 'squeak' their fingers in a bowl of dry cornflour and ask them to listen to the sound. What can they hear? Or ask 'Ooh, what's that funny noise?', 'What does it sound like?' The children then add dribbles of water and stir the cornflour to the consistency of thin cream – talk about changing consistency.

Hands in!

Handfuls of gluck can be run through the fingers (vocabulary – slimy, slidy, white and shiny).

Rolling the gluck into balls

The gluck will form into balls, but when the rolling action stops it reverses back into a runny consistency again. If the mixture is left to dry overnight in the bottom of a bowl it will crack and then the children can crumple it between their fingers. Rehydrate the mixture and ask questions such as, 'Where did the water go?' This enhances basic science learning, i.e. changing textures/properties by adding water.

Development

Add flavourings, e.g. vanilla, mint, cinnamon, curry powder and ask the children to guess the smell (out-of-date custard powder makes wonderful gluck too).

Threading/sewing

Resources

- Laces – the firm end of a lace can act as a needle in the first stages and save the children having to cope with a sharp point;
- Cards with punched holes or plastic shapes (animals or flowers) with specially designed with holes for early sewing;
- Long blunt needles with large eye holes;
- Wool, beads, lengths of drinking straws, buttons, pasta shapes;
- Embroidery hoops, pieces of material.

Activities such as threading a lace through shapes or wooden beads (a further development as holding a bead is harder than handling a plastic shape – the hole in the bead may also be smaller) need a strongly developed pincer grip and good visual perception. Staff should carefully note children who find this difficult and provide supporting activities such as picking up and replacing small objects.

Audai sewing a mat for Mum. Notice his tabard (see p. 48 for instructions on how to make)

Thread a large blunt needle with wool (staff should have a set number of needles ready threaded and check carefully that all the needles are returned after the activity). Link with the sorting tray which could have 'things to thread', e.g. lengths of coloured straw, pasta, beads, small pieces of material, so that each child has a necklace to take home. Tie wool around the needle at one end and through a large bead or piece of pasta at the other to stop the necklace pieces coming off.

As the children work, talk about the patterns they make: the colours, the sizes of beads that have been chosen and the kinds of materials which would thread easily.

Embroidery hoops

Fit pieces of material into the hoops, thread needles for the children and knot the end of the thread. Children can practise sewing patterns or attach other pieces of material or buttons. The hoop holds the material taut and so eases the task.

The next stage is for the children to sew canvas or material with holes (aida fabric). They are then ready to attempt the 'in and out pattern' of real sewing.

Sewing lavender bags

The younger children can make a simple lavender bag from a square of net gathered around a small mound of lavender and tied with a ribbon (see Fig. 5.2). The children who have learned to sew can make a lavender sachet.

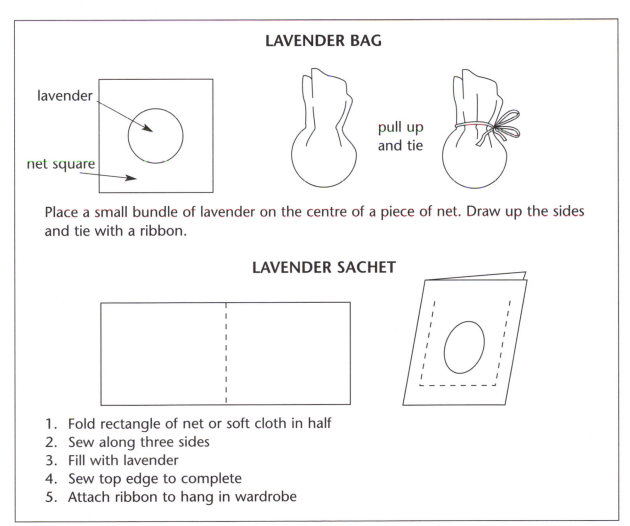

LAVENDER BAG

lavender

net square

pull up and tie

Place a small bundle of lavender on the centre of a piece of net. Draw up the sides and tie with a ribbon.

LAVENDER SACHET

1. Fold rectangle of net or soft cloth in half
2. Sew along three sides
3. Fill with lavender
4. Sew top edge to complete
5. Attach ribbon to hang in wardrobe

Figure 5.2 Making a lavender bag

Woodwork

Resources

- Goggles (these should be worn by every child who wishes to do woodwork);
- A variety of sizes of hammers and saws;
- A claw hammer to remove nails;
- Sandpaper – to sand away splinters before the children handle the wood;
- Thin pieces of soft wood (for sawing);
- A log for the nails;
- Nails of various lengths;
- A clamp for holding pieces of wood together;
- Small items which can be nailed onto the wood, e.g. pieces of material, thin linoleum, bottle tops, slices of cork to make wheels.

The dexterity needed for this activity will develop gradually so it should be designed in stages. Supervision is essential until the children's skill has been assessed and the staff are confident they are sufficiently proficient not to hurt themselves.

- Stage 1: Provide a large log (oversee and teach). Children enjoy tapping the nails in. Show them how to hold the hammer and the nails. Talk about careful action and tapping rather than banging!
- Stage 2: Children select and use individual pieces of wood – sawing or hammering pieces of material or thin wood onto the thicker pieces. Show them how to select the correct length of nail.
- Stage 3: Children can make a model then decorate it. As wood floats they could combine this with a water tray activity. Once modelling has begun, a clamp can hold pieces of wood together. Screwing up the clamp is a good activity for fine motor skill development.

Painting

Painting can be messy so tables need to be covered by newspapers or easily wiped plastic. The children can paint alone or with a friend if two sheets are fixed to the one side of an easel. They learn:

- to identify the different colours;
- how colours mix and blend to form others;
- to control the amount of paint on the brush;
- to control a brush (pre-writing skills);
- how to represent something they imagine or see.

Resources

- Bottle paint, palette paints;
- Cellulose paste – DO NOT USE WALLPAPER PASTE as this contains fungicides;
- Powder paint – white and colours;
- Washing powder (non-bio);
- Different types of brushes (chubby, chunky or long and fine) give different experiences in controlling the brush, thus helping the development of fine motor skills as well as creating different effects on the paper;
- Paint tubs and lids;
- Large tray for finger or leaf printing;

- Items for printing, e.g. bath puffs, pieces of sponge;
- Sticks for mixing.

Mixing the paint

This should be done with the children's help! To produce the correct consistency of paint:

Children put 2 tablespoons of cellulose paste into every pot and add 1 teaspoon washing powder and 2 tablespoons powder paint.
Adults add a small splash of water or children add two tablespoonfuls.
Children mix until smooth.

Adults and children together discuss the change in colour and texture of the mixture. Pastel colours can be obtained by mixing in 1 tablespoon of white paint powder. Primary colours mixed together give other shades, so the children learn about the effects of blending.

Other activities

The children can spread the paint over the base of a large tray and make patterns with their fingers or with other tools. After washing their hands they can take a print and transfer this pattern onto paper. When several children do this together, they can compare hand sizes, count fingers, identify 'fingers close together and spread out wide' etc. They can use their feet to make footprints along a roll of paper and see how the marks get fainter as the paint is used up. They can count the footsteps and talk about the instep (if this is obvious).

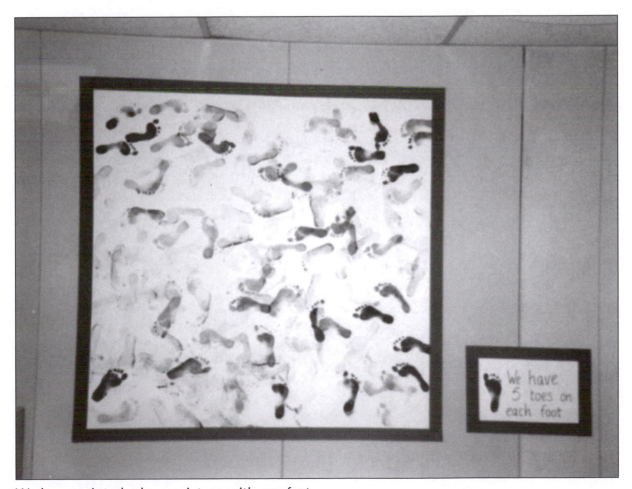

We have painted a large picture with our feet

Link with an environment theme

> Winter – look at the snow to see tracks;
> Autumn – use leaves to make prints;
> Farm visit – look at the footprints of different animals on a muddy path.

Exploring textures

Again using the large paint tray, the children can experiment with different materials, e.g. bath puffs, cotton wool, sponge rollers and spreaders, a piece of corduroy etc. They can then discover:

- if and how different materials absorb paint;
- what kinds of prints they make;
- the patterns that can be made by using different items.

Organisation and learning about routine

Painting provides an excellent opportunity for the children to learn quite a complex routine. They can be involved from deciding on the activity to cleaning up. What do they need to understand?

1. Aprons on (where they are kept and where they are put after use);
2. How many children can paint at once (the number of aprons controls this);
3. That they should name their work;
4. That they must take turns in having the large/small brush or roller;
5. That they must respect others and their work if they are producing something together;
6. That spills have to be mopped up quickly (how to do it);
7. That paint pots, brushes and rollers have to be cleaned and put away in the correct place;
8. That their work needs to placed somewhere safe to dry and they may have to wait until tomorrow to take it home! (Delayed gratification can be difficult.)

Development

Once these basic instructions can be followed, the children can produce a group picture (small groups can do this in turn). Outdoor painting can be carried out successfully in groups if a long roll of paper is held down by large stones. This can then be taken indoors to make a lovely wall display or a 'tablecloth' for a nature table.

Baking and cooking

Children love to bake and cook, especially if they are making something for others to share. A great deal of mathematical learning is involved, e.g. counting spoonfuls, estimating 'how many more', as well as science, e.g. weighing and balancing (pan scales are recommended), noting the change in textures caused by heat or cold etc. Cooking and baking skills are also important activities of daily living; perhaps this generation needs to learn them more than older children who ate less processed food.

Safety and hygiene

The cooker must be positioned in a permanently cordoned-off area where the children cannot gain access. Baking aprons should be kept specifically for cooking activities and not used as painting aprons!

Learning through preparing the snack

The children prepare snack as much as possible. There are many opportunities for pouring, spreading, cutting, passing plates and mugs and learning the social niceties of eating together.

The children select cards from an alphabetical list to match the food they have that day. Numbers often appear that tell the children how many pieces of each they should have. This means that counting is important – especially if the food is a favourite one.

Samantha and Chloë spread their toast for their snack

Dionne and Josh enjoy their snacks. Note the children's recipe books and the alphabetical list of snack items. These can be laminated to withstand sticky fingers.

At the snack preparation area, children's recipe books (e.g. how to make a banana sandwich) are laid alongside the bread and fruit (bananas can be cut into chunks but not removed from their skins to save discoloration). Apples are quartered and placed in bowls of diluted orange. At tasting time, it can be appropriate to compare, for example, an avocado pear with an ordinary pear in terms of size, shape, colour and the size of stone as well as taste. In the nursery, no opportunity for hands-on learning is missed!

Hygiene is very important. Many children think that if their hands don't look grubby, they are clean, so establishing a routine from the outset saves chivvying and checking later on. Planning the timing of everything is crucial: buns should be cool enough to taste before story or soup is ready to enjoy before the end of the session, and washing up afterwards is also a important part of the routine.

Ideally the children should bake in groups of four at a time so only four aprons should be made available. This small number allows them to have individual bowls and have a lot of responsibility for the work. Larger groups mean that the children only get the opportunity for a few stirs before passing the bowl on, thereby limiting the involvement of fine motor skills; they do not get the same sense of ownership, of having made something really worthwhile 'by myself!'

Resources

- An old-fashioned pan balance scale for weighing lets the children estimate amounts and see the quantities needed to make the pans balance;
- 2 small pans/cooking pots;
- 4 individual bowls, 4 mixing spoons, jugs for liquid;
- Wooden spoons;
- Dry ingredients as appropriate;
- Knives (adult and children's) to cut vegetables which have been prepared into finger-sized chunks;
- Scone cutters of various sizes and shapes. Children choose and name, e.g. 'I'd like a small square, red one';
- A flour sieve;
- Rolling pins (dowel rod or a broom handle can be cut to size). These must be kept separately from those used for dough or clay activities;
- A mouli grater for cheese lets the children turn the handle as a member of staff holds the lid down;
- 2 × 18cm tins (for birthday sponges) and airing trays for cooling;
- Bun trays;
- Table-top (candle) warmers – these have sufficient heat to melt small quantities of fat for bird cakes or chocolate for crispies (not too often!). Select those which have a solid top with holes because small fingers can poke through those that have a wire grid. It is also easier to balance the small pans on a solid base.

Recipes

Choose recipes that will allow the children to do nearly all the work themselves: scones, biscuits, buns, pizza and soup are all suitable. Staff can support the children in making simple, illustrated recipe books which they can use (almost) independently. If these are laminated, they withstand spills and doughy fingers staining the leaves as they find their place!

A favourite recipe folder can be added to the parents' notice board so that they can continue baking or cooking at home if the children show an interest in doing so.

Scones (plain, cheese, honey or fruit)
Weigh the whole quantity then split between four bowls:
56gm margarine or butter
1 dessert spoon sugar
227gm self-raising flour
milk to mix

1 egg
a small handful of sultanas, some grated cheese or a spoon of honey (optional extras)
1 teaspoon baking powder

Method
Sieve dry ingredients together
Grease baking trays, if not non-stick
Rub in margarine or butter
Break egg into cup and mix with milk
Add to dry mixture
Roll out and cut with selected shape cutter
Bake at gas mark 7/425°F/220°C for 12 minutes

Shortbread
168gm plain flour
115gm margarine
56gm sugar

Method
Mix margarine and sugar together until creamy
Gradually add flour
Knead, then cut into fingers
Bake at gas mark 4/350°F/180°C for 10–15 minutes

Making a birthday cake

A memorable way to celebrate a child's birthday is to appoint him or her the 'chief baker' when making a cake! The birthday child is given all the important jobs, e.g. choosing the three helpers, mixing the icing, distributing the slices and taking part of the cake home to share with the family.

Four children with a bowl each require:
56gm margarine or butter
56gm caster sugar
1 egg
2 tablespoons (56gm) self-raising flour
jam to stick the cakes together
³/₄ cup white icing sugar (do not use food colourings in case of allergies)
candles and number/decoration for the top

Activity	Teaching points
Weigh the butter. Mix till soft.	Talk about more/less needed to balance
Weigh the sugar. Mix into butter.	Listen to the noise as the sugar is added
Each child weighs an egg and mixes it in their bowl.	Talk about hens laying eggs.
Weigh the flour. Sieve and gently fold into the mixture.	Talk about the reasons for sieving flour (no lumps, adding air).

Staff should combine the mixtures from the four bowls ready to divide into two halves of the sponge. The children should grease and flour the two sponge tins, then divide and smooth the mixture equally.

Activity	Teaching points
Staff then put the cakes in the oven and set the timer (20 mins @ gas mark 5/375°F/190°C). The children are not allowed near the oven	Talk about how long the cake will take to cook and cool
While the cakes are cooking the birthday child makes the icing by adding one teaspoon of water at a time to the icing sugar	Talk about the changing consistency and colour of the icing (the white powder turns grey when water is added)

While the icing is setting, the birthday child counts out the correct number of candles and selects the correct 'Happy Birthday – 3 Today' or 'Happy Birthday – 4 Today' decoration for the top.

Today Dionne is the birthday girl. She is four

As the cake arrives to the assembled group, the birthday child can tell everyone what he or she enjoyed on his or her birthday. The other children have to guess the child's age from counting the candles before they are lit. The birthday child then blows them out and makes a wish!

Making a bird cake

Use a solid vegetable fat as animal fats can have an unpleasant smell. Wild bird seed contains nuts to which some children may be allergic; finch mix is nut-free and therefore more suitable. Porridge oats are also ideal as they can also be used for cooking porridge or biscuits another day, thus allowing the children to taste the oats too. Use yoghurt pots to contain the cakes and nets (from punnets of fruit) with ribbons to tie them to the trees.

Dionne and Kiera are following the recipe for making bird cakes

Page 1: Wash your hands. Put on an apron

Page 2: A teacher will light the candle

Page 3: Melt 1 spoonful of fat

Page 4: Add 1 spoonful of oats and 1 spoonful of seed

Page 5: Mix together

Page 6: Put in a pot

Page 7: Put in the fridge

Although adult supervision is needed as a lit candle is being used, children will quickly be able to follow the booklet and make their own bird cake. This experience lets the children appreciate the cycle of solid fat melting (application of heat) and becoming firm again when the mixture is cooled. The chilled mixture can then be turned out of the pots and strung up in nets tied to a tree (or a rope if there are no suitable trees available).

Making soup

Making a vegetable soup is quite easy and the children can also make pumpkin soup for Hallowe'en (after making lanterns). Any available vegetables can be used, e.g. carrots (the tops can be grown in saucers of water), turnips, potatoes, peas, leeks etc., plus cold water and a vegetable stock cube.

Activity	Teaching points
Children should help to wash the vegetables	Explain where the vegetables were grown; which parts were under the ground. Discuss colour, texture and size
Adults should cut the vegetables into chip-size pieces and the children can do the final chopping under adult supervision	Let the children taste the raw vegetables. Demonstrate how to hold the knife and show the size required
Add the vegetable stock cube (this can be dissolved in a cup in a small amount of warm water)	Explain how the stock cube melts and adds flavour to the soup

An adult can add boiling water to the mixture to speed up the cooking process providing the kitchen is closed off from the children.

Pumpkin soup

This is a great favourite with the children which they enjoy telling the families about. It uses the flesh of the pumpkin which has been cut out to make lanterns (see photo above). The seeds can be dried in the oven and either eaten or used at the gluing table.

1lb pumpkin flesh
1 onion
1 bay leaf
$1/_2$ teaspoon cumin
1 pint of stock (made with a vegetable cube)

Children chop the flesh and the onion. All ingredients then go in the pot to simmer for 30 minutes. Remove the bay leaf, blend or sieve it, then enjoy!

The children helped to set up this Hallowe'en display. The pumpkin flesh was made into soup.

Brandon and Keith make a spell for Hallowe'en　Shaquelle dooks (bobs) for his apple

Making music

Use either bought or home-made tuned and untuned percussion (see p. 51). At first allow the children to experiment with different pieces of percussion to find out about the kind of sound each makes.

The children can accompany either a tape of short pieces of music, e.g. nursery rhymes, or an adult playing an instrument. As the aim is simply to have the children begin and finish at the same time as the other music, it helps if they have already sung the song or know the tune. If a tape is used, an adult can beat out the rhythm with a beater to help them recognise that there is a regular beat underlying the tune, although at this early stage enjoyment rather than musicality is the aim!

Use a variety of background music, e.g. a gentle lullaby and contrasting marching songs. The children have to play quietly or loudly as appropriate. Talk with the children about the quality of the music and its purpose, e.g. the lullaby is for soothing and rocking the baby to sleep while the marching music has a strong beat to keep everyone in step. Some children can march and 'halt' at the correct time, while others accompany the tape by beating out the rhythm on their drums.

Creating their own music

Many children will be confident enough to experiment and make their own music without a backing track. Some enjoy singing to accompany themselves. It gives them real pleasure if their music can be tape-recorded and played back – a video is even better! Sometimes children like to dance to their own or their friends' music.

Listening to stories to music

Children enjoy different approaches to story time and playing music such as *Peter and the Wolf* or *The Teddy Bears' Picnic* adds variety and interest. Some records, e.g. *Jack and the Beanstalk*, tell the story slowly, giving the children time to try out the actions such as planting the beans or chopping down the beanstalk.

Each story can last for several days – the children may suggest ways of joining in with their own instrument or they may want to dance to a particular tune. Music develops a sense of rhythm which is important in learning to move and learning to read, as well as the more obvious training in listening to the music and appreciating the quality of the sound.

Gardening and growing

Safety in the garden

Each morning staff must check the garden for broken glass or even syringes which could have been thrown in overnight. Close examination under hedges is essential.

A shallow garden pond can be a wonderful habitat for minibeasts but secure netting is essential and staff have to be vigilant at all times. If the garden is small, then staff have to decide whether a pond is the best resource available.

Resources for designing the garden

- Planting: if it is possible to start the garden from scratch, choose plants carefully. They should be at their best when the children are in nursery, not flowering during the holidays. Try to choose vigorous plants which show the seasons and the cycle of plant life, e.g. snowdrops and crocus for the spring; marigolds, lavender and stocks for summer; fuchsias and rock roses for the autumn and winter-flowering pansies for the cold months.
- A beech hedge which has leaves that change colour and fall – providing materials for leaf prints and sweeping-up activities in the garden – is a much better resource than say a privet (evergreen) hedge which never changes, although it does provide food for the stick insects!
- Raised beds and smooth paths are essential for children in wheelchairs. They also give variety to the layout of the garden and can stimulate discussions on the heights of different plants and their suitability for the raised beds.
- Flower tubs and pots can be planted by the children. If they plant layers of different bulbs with other surface plants on top there will always be colour throughout the seasons (see Figure 5.3). In warm weather especially the tubs must be well watered – a job which the children love to do!
- Herb pots: a tub of aromatic herbs is a wonderful resource as the senses (smell and taste as well as sight) can be involved. The children need to understand that these are the only plants in the garden that can be eaten (apart from lettuces, radishes and tomatoes etc. grown in a vegetable plot – in Scotland outdoor tomatoes are not a good choice as they don't ripen in time for the children to enjoy them and need watering over the summer break).
- Mini-pots: yoghurt cartons make splendid individual seed beds. An individual crocus corm or some sunflower seeds can be taken home by each child so that they can be responsible for watering and watching/relating the changes that occur! Seeds from apples or avocados eaten in the nursery can be grown in pots. Cress grows easily on lint or kitchen paper; this shows a different growing medium and the changes can be readily observed. The fast growth will help to retain the children's enthusiasm and interest. Similarly, hyacinths can be grown in water in special see-through pots so that the children can observe the growth of the root system. They also learn about keeping the bulb in the dark and watching the changes so that they know when to bring it into the light to flower.

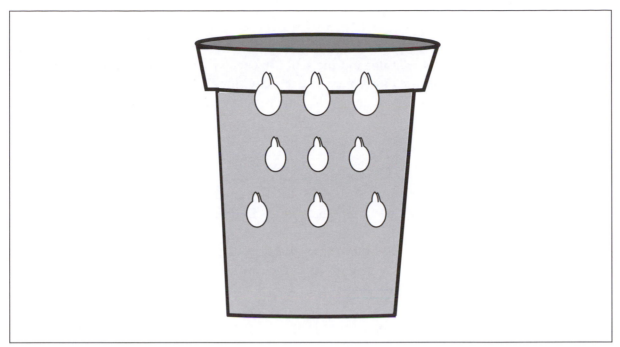

Figure 5.3 Planting layers of different bulbs with other surface plants on top will provide year-round colour

Providing a habitat for minibeasts

A fallen tree trunk or an undisturbed log pile (especially if there is some rotting wood) will encourage minibeasts such as slaters, centipedes and worms which are a great source of wonder and learning for the children. They can be lifted into a magnifying box for study but staff need to ensure they are released quickly and carefully. The children can look closely, see lots of detail and learn the meaning of words such as fragile.

The minibeasts may be kept for a short while in a fish tank prepared with fresh earth and stones provided it is kept moist and there is appropriate food.

A well-stocked garden can provide many resources for the gluing table, e.g. leaves, seed heads, flower heads. Some children are attracted by stones and bring them into the nursery to paint.

Outdoor play

In good weather, many nursery activities can take place outside. This is especially important if the children live in high rise flats where access to outdoor play may be limited.

Provision of suitable clothing

In winter, a stock of hats and gloves is necessary for those who don't have their own and in summer, sun hats are essential.

Notice on parents' notice board

Parents should be requested to apply sun cream before the children come to nursery and to supply an appropriate hat, when necessary.

Shelter

If it is very sunny, using beach shelters to provide shade is a good idea as they are quickly and easily assembled – tents get very stuffy and the staff can't see what is going on inside! Bringing the children inside at intervals for a story may be necessary (they can stay outside if shade is available), as are extra drinks – possibly using ice the children have made the day before.

Moving equipment outside

- If the water tray is moved out of doors and placed on the ground, staff must be extra vigilant in case a child falls in. One member must stay by the tray and not have his or her attention diverted by children using other equipment. Young children have been known to drown in only one inch of water.
- Painting activities can take place by taking a long roll of paper outside with the ends held down with wooden blocks (rather than move all the easels). The children enjoy another experience using large brushes, palette paints and tubs of water. They learn about evaporation as their paintings dry in the sun.
- The house corner teaset should be left inside and a separate picnic set kept for the garden.

Shopping

Taking the children shopping needs careful planning. Beforehand, discuss what is needed and what shops should be visited. Smaller, specialist shops can be quite revealing for children who usually only visit supermarkets. The teacher can point out the butcher, the baker etc. and highlight what each sells. This can then link with making shopping lists in the house corner.

Make a list with the children – some children can draw items that are needed.

Traffic safety

This could be a follow-up to a visit by the local police officer in the 'People who help us' theme. Practise crossing the road carefully with adults holding hands – children should never be allowed to cross the road alone even if they claim their parents/carers allow them to do so.

Walking to the shops

The aim here is to alert children to all the things they pass, e.g. flowers, trees, spiders' webs, fancy ironwork on gates, different doors, heights of buildings, library, road crossings etc. The children also enjoy playing spotting games such as 'my number' or 'my letter' as they walk along.

Large construction

Safety considerations are vital in this area. There should be a designated floor space, preferably a corner so that through traffic is avoided and if bricks topple they are less likely to hurt any child. The area can be 'sealed off' by cupboards to store the blocks (to avoid them being carried into other areas of the nursery) and allow easy retrieval. It is a good idea to paint a red line around the area at the children's shoulder height and explain to them that no building is allowed above this height.

Supervision is essential as sometimes children will try to climb on the structures they have made – these are likely to be insecure until the children learn what will and what won't work!

Organisation

Sometimes this area can be very busy and numbers may have to be restricted to say four children at a time. However, some of the children may have constructed a fort which can safely house more (with supervision of course). A hard and fast rule of 'four only' may stifle creativity.

Handling the large bricks and placing them carefully is excellent for the development of motor skills (coordination, balance and control in picking up and letting go). Large bricks of various lengths and widths present problem-solving challenges which develop the children's perception of shape and size, and if/how things fit together.

Hard hats

The children enjoy being real workers and hard hats help them get into role and begin to make them aware of safety considerations in the outdoor areas. They can be worn with workers' yellow, 'don't knock me down' overvests.

Discussions on how other jobs need safety equipment too can be useful (firefighters have breathing apparatus; lollipop men/women have white coats and luminous strips). Sometimes children do not realise that adults need to take safety precautions too.

Small block construction

This area allows the children to handle and build with different shapes of blocks which they have been learning about at the gluing table. Staff should always use the correct mathematical language, e.g. cylinder, cuboids, spheres, cubes. Cubes are particularly important as there are few examples of real cubes in the nursery.

Corbinn and Scott are busy constructing at the low table

Storage

Ice cream tubs can be named with each shape and the children should learn to replace them correctly when they have finished their work or at tidy-up time. Smaller items can be stored in a divided tray with a picture of the item glued to the bottom of the section to speed up correct storage and prevent 'Where shall I put it?' questions.

This area is excellent for the development of fine motor skills where two hands have to work together at the midline of the body. Perception of shape and size, comparison of shapes (which ones will fit?), aesthetic development (which colours go together?), learning about design and pattern are all implicit in this activity. By trial and error of selecting and rejecting, the children also develop their estimating skills.

Construction kits

There are many kits on the market to encourage construction. These are expensive but will contain items such as plastic nuts and bolts and connecting rods not easily obtained elsewhere (see 'Catalogues', p. 110 for suppliers).

A large low table (available from Argos @ approx. £40) is invaluable for construction and playing with small world toys. The low-level flat surface is at the correct height for kneeling; it is large enough for several children to join in thereby encouraging cooperative play. If shelves are positioned nearby, the components can be stored quickly in the correct place.

Puzzles and games

A range of puzzles and games, and matching and sorting activities of different levels of challenge should always be available. Jigsaws with different numbers and sizes of pieces can be self-selected. These can be rotated to hold interest and sometimes matched to the prevailing theme, e.g. farmyard animals or shops or seasonal pictures.

The younger children may need to begin with the inset puzzles which are excellent for visual appreciation of shape as well as giving practice in using the pincer grip to manipulate the pieces into place. This is so important for emergent writing.

6 Observation/assessment/recording, intervention and identifying/ supporting children with difficulties

Observation

One of the nursery staff's most important tasks is to compile an accurate assessment profile for each child. From the start, an efficient and effective method of recording, filing and analysing observations needs to be established so that the profile contains the most pertinent information to support the child.

Observation is at the heart of nursery practice – 'watching, listening and talking' are key to getting to know and understand each child. Staff are constantly observing children across all aspects of their development so that they can monitor each child's progress.

Dated observations

Dated observations are essential as they provide 'evidence' of the child's participation, competence and progress over a range of activities. This essential information will:

- guide staff in planning learning activities which will offer the correct level of challenge or reinforcement for each child;
- provide material for 'profiling', used for reporting home and/or to outside agencies and for transition documents to primary school;
- provide 'evidence' of children showing any signs of delay, having specific difficulties, or even outstanding abilities. This data can give psychologists, physiotherapists or speech therapists a fuller picture than they could obtain on just a one-off visit or by carrying out a single test. The recordings will also prevent time wasted by replicating observations;
- alert staff to the best new resources to buy.

Why record all this detail?

New staff may ask, 'Why have things to be written when I know what each child can do?' But once they see how these recordings form the basis of staff planning discussions about how best to support each child and provide the most appropriate resources to take their learning forward, they realise that they cannot rely on memory alone to store all the details for several children over time! Inconclusive comments such as, 'Well, I think that maybe . . .' are not really very helpful and important information would not be available if staff are away from the nursery for any reason (sick leave or holidays). This could result in delayed support for the child.

These details are the key pieces of information which will 'prove' that the child is either progressing, staying still or even regressing over time which is why dating each observation and filing them in order is so critically important. Recordings can also stimulate valuable discussions if, for example, the staff 'see' different things in one child. This is perfectly possible given the different opportunities each member of staff has had for practice and the fact that children's level of competence can fluctuate from day to day. Sometimes children surprise by leaping ahead and making significant progress quickly while at other times they seem to be on a plateau, needing a long time to practise the skills they have achieved rather than learning any more. Some children have prodigious memories for detail while others with poor, short-term memories often forget what they have been able to do the day before. This may be due to lack of motivation and interest in a particular activity, rather than an inability to recall, but in the nursery where there the children are able to make choices, this is less likely to be the cause. It is important to note this as one observation in an accumulation which will be the focus of regular, even daily, staff discussions.

Any observation which causes surprise will alert the staff to focus on that particular aspect of behaviour in future observations, followed up by joint decisions about ways to challenge or support the child.

Case study: Gemma

The staff were delighted, but surprised, when a student, Lynn, recorded that Gemma could recognise her name. Lynn had observed Gemma at snack where she had confidently selected her name from the wall and so she awarded her a tick in the 'can recognise own name' box in the assessment file. The staff advised Lynn to widen her field of observation – and indeed when Gemma tried to find her name at the painting table she was lost. At snack she had used the colour of the card to make her choice. Lynn realised that one observation should be backed up by others before drawing any conclusions.

Seemingly 'out of character' incidents would also be noted but not necessarily recorded in any formal document unless there were signs that they could become habitual.

Case study: Gordon

Normally, four-year-old Gordon was a sunny-natured child – open, friendly and the apple of his mother's eye. Anticipating the arrival of his new brother or sister, the staff had set out a baby corner, which Gordon ignored. The idea of being the 'big brother' didn't seem to give him any pleasure, nor did her arrival! The baby's homecoming coincided with Gordon crying and scowling, not wanting to stay at nursery and being unpleasant to the other children. The staff were patient and understanding in the hope that this phase would soon pass.

Sadly it didn't, and approaching transition time, he still hadn't reverted to his earlier happier frame of mind. His new reluctance was also affecting his learning and his level of participation – there was a huge discrepancy between what the staff knew he could do and what he was now prepared to do. This provided a dilemma as to the most helpful information to pass on to the next stage.

Making observations

It is not always easy to make accurate observations as many of the things children choose to do are over in a flash! With movement problems especially, it can be difficult to describe exactly what is amiss. One answer is to video record the children (with parental permission) so that replays and pauses and discussions with other staff can clarify any doubts. The film might also be passed to outside experts as another form of evidence when requesting extra support.

There are various other ways of recording observations, the best being those that are quick and meaningful, pointing to 'ways to help'. Some nurseries prefer to collect information about any small developments, e.g. a child using a more complex sentence than previously, one child offering to share with another, a child naming a colour correctly, climbing on the frame for the first time or concentrating for a longer spell in a particular area. For some children even being able to sit or stand still is a sign of real progress because being able to concentrate and pay attention (in order to learn) often depends on this skill.

Staff can record these kinds of observations on sticky labels from a roll, fixed on a clipboard or concealed in a pocket (see Fig. 6.1). Some staff find the clipboard cumbersome and less readily available than the roll, while others prefer having a firm base for their recordings – different ways can be tried. If each observation is named, dated and headed to match each developmental area, then it can be added quickly to the prepared file in date order for consideration when several observations have been made. Being meticulous in dating and date ordering saves confusion when analysing the information for profiling.

> Robbie B. 28/8/02 Phys. Dev. and Movement
>
> Keen to pedal trike but still pushing with both feet.
> Unable to coordinate pushing with one foot.

> Robbie B. 4/9/02 Phys. Dev. and Movement
>
> R. pedalled the trike for the first time today. Very keen to
> share this achievement with Mum.

> Anne 9/9/02 Com. and Lit.
>
> Still finding difficulty in making herself understood. Speak
> to Mum and raise the possibility of speech therapy.
> Becoming more reluctant to try to speak.

> Caitlin 4/10/02 Cr., Exp. and Aes.
>
> Spent 20 mins at the glue table creating TV set for house
> corner. Knew exactly what she wanted to achieve. Adult
> help required for cuttting card.

> Shannon 11/10/02 Com. and Lang.
>
> Shannon reads her name in different contexts now. She
> sequenced the days of the week (elephant collage) for
> the first time today.

Figure 6.1 Examples of sticky label observations

The observations file

These observations should be accumulated in specially organised files. Five A4 files are required to store information on the following groups:

1. AM girls
2. AM boys
3. PM girls
4. PM boys
5. Full-timers

Each folder has a numbered list of the children's names at the front, thereafter the folder is sub-divided by coloured dividers so that each child has his or her own section of five headed pages. Each page within each child's section is headed to match the framework document (DfEE 2000; HMI 1997), i.e. emotional, social, and personal (ESPD), communication and language (C & L), physical and motor development (Phys. Dev.), knowledge and understanding of the world (K & U) and expressive and aesthetic development (Exp. and Aes). This system allows for quick and easy insertion of the sticky labels or notes into the correct place, as well as providing an ongoing, accurate record if immediate information is required by a parent, head teacher or an inspector. Everyone can be confident in making suggestions for strategies to help or recommendations for the most appropriate resources.

Avoiding duplication

Some organisation is needed to avoid different members of staff recording the same information about the same children. One strategy is to provide checklists (see Fig. 6.2).

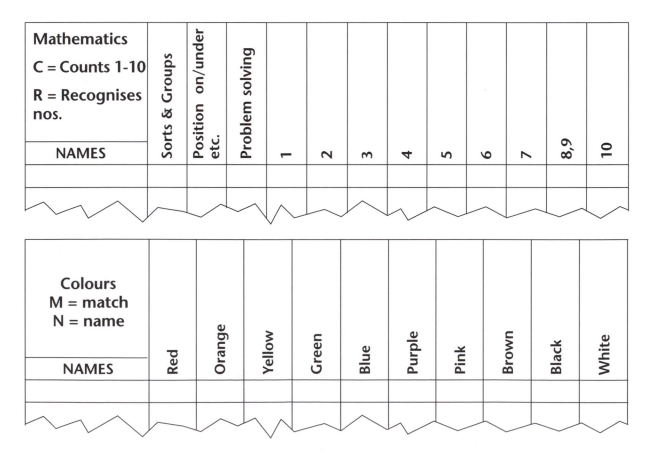

Figure 6.2 Checklist sheets. Some examples

Knowledge and Understanding of the World NAMES	Observes and Investigates	Uses senses	Interest in minibeasts/themes	Appreciates other people's jobs	Understands properties of some materials	Cares for plants and pets at home	Recognises patterns and shapes	Asks questions	Sequences	Understands own growth	Understands personal safety

Writing, Drawing, Reading NAMES	Draws	Draws detail	Writes	Writes symbols	Some sounds	Knows name	Writes name	Looks at books	Finds information in books	Makes rhymes	Controls pencil

Listening and Talking NAMES	Listens at play	Listens at story	Responds to story	Responds to rhyme	Follows instructions	Short conversations	Longer conversations	Discusses experiences	Talks in role play	Retells a story	Expresses needs/feelings	Fun with language

Physical Development and Movement NAMES	Plays energetically	Controls body balance	Spatial awareness	Can crawl	Uses spinning cone	Can control scissors	Pincer grip	Pencil grip	Ball skills	Catch, throw	Uses pole	Can run and jump

Figure 6.2 Checklist sheets - continued

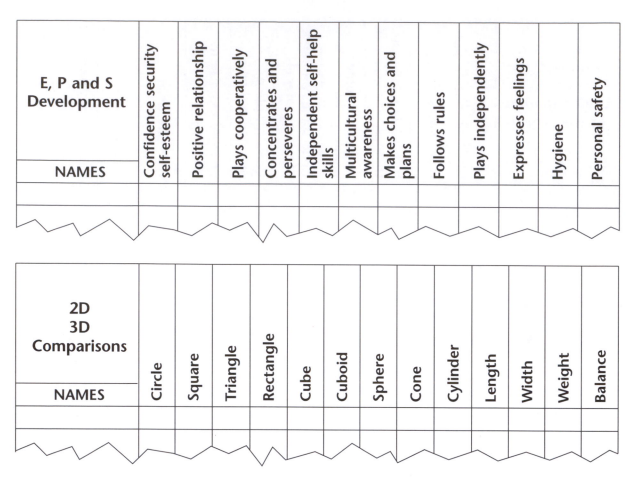

E, P and S Development NAMES	Confidence security self-esteem	Positive relationship	Plays cooperatively	Concentrates and perseveres	Independent self-help skills	Multicultural awareness	Makes choices and plans	Follows rules	Plays independently	Expresses feelings	Hygiene	Personal safety

2D 3D Comparisons NAMES	Circle	Square	Triangle	Rectangle	Cube	Cuboid	Sphere	Cone	Cylinder	Length	Width	Weight	Balance

Figure 6.2 Checklist sheets - continued

The children's names are listed down one side and the targets arranged along the top so that a grid is formed. During an activity, the staff set out to observe the particular competences which have been identified in advance rather than noting small incidental things (as happens using the sticky label method). This avoids duplication which can occur when different staff record the same observation on sticky labels, but concentrating on specific targets only can also result on other interesting happenings being missed. The recordings from the checklists are transferred into a master copy for the class.

The symbols 'O', '/' or '★' point to different levels of competence, shorthand for recording 'can't do', 'nearly there' or 'can do'. The date should be entered into the box when the target is achieved. These recordings give an immediate visual picture of each child's competence against set criteria. Again dating is vitally important so that progress is monitored accurately.

The checklists also show:

- if a child has been missed being observed for a particular competence in which case one member of staff would be assigned to rectify that omission.
- the general level of competence across the group. This shows whether individual or more general support is needed.
- the pace of subsequent input. If all the children quickly achieve the set criterion then the pace of learning can be increased or a more challenging one can be substituted. On the other hand, if only one or two succeed then more reinforcement is needed. Perhaps one particular competence is holding up progress for several children, e.g. recognition of colours. Then stress on each colour would be built into the teaching plan (perhaps as a substitute) or 'learning colours' could become a nursery–wide theme.

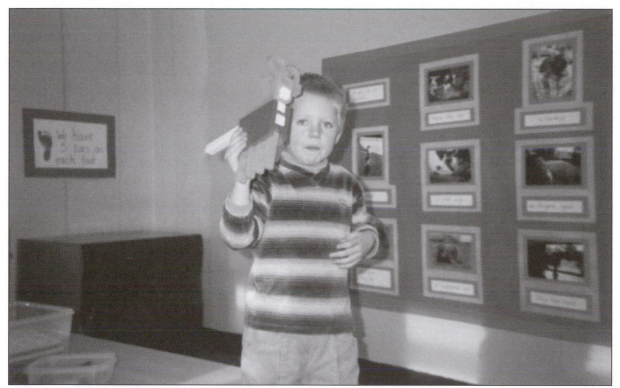

Keith is learning about green and yellow

All of this observation, recording and analysis needs careful organisation, with all members of staff clear about what they have to do. But once the strategy is in place, it works! It provides accurate, up-to-the-minute information for a range of important purposes including profiling and transition documentation, thus providing confidence that a sound job is being done.

Intervention

Yes or no?

There are several tricky questions which need to be thought through before intervention takes place. The question of whether or not staff should intervene in children's work and play or have the confidence to leave them alone is much more complex than it sounds.

Adults often feel they should be 'doing something' – after all, that is why they are being paid is it not? But unless that 'something' is timely and relevant, it can be the very thing that stops the children's play or prevents them from finding the solution to any problem themselves. This deprives them of the joy of discovery and puts the adults back in charge. The children may then realise that they are no longer in control of their game and withdraw, or they may stay but wait for more adult direction. Once the adults have taken over the responsibility of leading the development, they cannot then abandon it! If the activity is to be completed, the adults have to keep on making suggestions as to how this is to be done.

It is not easy to observe and understand what children are aiming to do and they may not wish to interrupt their play to explain – indeed, they may not have the language to do so. One of the most important things nursery staff can develop is the confidence to stay back and observe. This is not 'doing nothing'; this is a considered choice. It could be the best one until they are sure they can justify intervening and know how to do it well.

Cohen (1997) is one author who is desperately concerned by adults' willingness to interfere. He asks, 'How can we, long out of practice oldies, tell children how to play?' And when he hears of adults taking over and making suggestions how to play better, he explodes, 'Are there social engineers on the swings?' Perhaps if the strategy was called interference rather than intervention, adults would be more willing to wait and see. Yet other educationalists, e.g. Bennett *et al.* 1999 assert that intervention is a good thing and that without it some children will never progress as they should. He explains that these children will do the same (perhaps unproductive) things over and over again but not become more skilful at all.

Perhaps this claim gives the first clue as to what evidence would support intervention, i.e. that the observed child, over several observations, was 'practising' aimlessly and not progressing. Even this needs to be handled with care.

Reasons for intervention: questions worth considering

Questions about non-participation

- *Do the children just need time to stand and stare?* After all, the nursery environment can be over-whelming and periods of 'chilling out' can help energy to be recouped. Or perhaps the start of the day at home has been fraught for some reason and the children need time to calm down and settle into the nursery routine. Piaget (1964) claims that all young children are intrinsically motivated to learn and that they will progress at a pace which suits their capacity so to do. He denies that any child would be lazy and suggests that any non-participation would have another cause. He claims that if adults take over and force the child to learn new things, he or she may do so, but this would result in rote or surface learning. In this kind of learning, the meaning is not understood and so it doesn't transfer to a different situation, i.e. it is of limited use.

- *Are these children playing aimlessly but at the same time watching another activity carefully?* If so, they may well be 'learning without doing'. They may need time to observe to work out strategies for getting into a group to play, or they may be learning the rules of a game from some distance away. Perhaps they may simply need time to observe all the children to find a role model or consider all the activities in the nursery before making their choice. If learning is going on, albeit at some distance, no intervention is required. Some nurseries, recognising this need, provide a 'look-out post', perhaps a rocking horse or some other vantage point. They recognise how valuable this kind of observation time can be! The duration of this non-active participation, however, would be an important part of the staff's observation and recording policy (another reason for dating observations), and intervention strategies would have to be considered if this went on too long. What can be done, obviously depends on the reason behind the child's reluctance to participate. If the child doesn't have the confidence to join in, perhaps a friendly child could be persuaded to suggest a quiet game. Or perhaps the child would relish helping a member of staff to find a book for story time and be praised for his or her choice. Sometimes allocating small areas of responsibility and providing deserved praise can break down a barrier and give the children confidence to overcome their fears.

- *Is repeated practice with one toy or piece of equipment providing security or demonstrating obsessive behaviour?* If the latter is the case, staff have to try to find ways of extending the children's choices. Removing the toy would only cause frustration and unhappiness – or possibly an explosion which upsets everyone – so this is not an option. If, for example, one child appears obsessed by a red car, then providing a garage with another red car inside might just encourage him to extend his play. This could simply be placed near the child with no comment in the first instance, so that he doesn't feel threatened by extra attention. If there is still no improvement after the child has settled and been given a lot of support, nursery staff should consider seeking expert help. This behaviour might indicate the presence of Asperger's syndrome and special guidance may be needed.

Questions about safety

- *Is danger looming?* A second, critically important reason for intervention is where safety is concerned and there should be no hesitation – immediate intervention is required! Sometimes games get out of hand and squabbles arise, or a child's frustration turns into aggression, threatening the other children or the equipment. Staff have to intervene to cool things down – if possible by distracting the angry children and involving them in another interesting activity. Confrontation should always be avoided as children cannot listen to reasoned explanations while they are upset. Given a little time, these can be given calmly and hopefully the difficulties can be resolved and friendships resumed.

'Catch them being good or anticipate and avert flare-ups in a positive way' is the best advice any teacher can have. If this doesn't work, however, a 'time-out chair' can keep the perpetrator aside until things have settled down – but remember he or she is there!

- *Have small resources been misused?* Despite close observation of the children as they play/work, and attempts to match the resources which are provided to the children's level of responsibility, some will decide to poke beads or pieces of pasta up their noses, prod other children with paint brushes or fail to take sufficient care at the large apparatus or the woodwork bench. Immediate intervention is essential. While one member of staff deals with the incident, the remaining staff have to cover the gap that has been left – gathering the children together for a story is one way of coping!

Staying with the task

A third justifiable reason for intervening is to try to encourage children to stay with an activity for some time. While the three-year-olds can wander off quite freely – even if this does devastate the staff who have spent ages supporting them – a short attention span is the norm and therefore expected in these very young children. Staying with a task to complete it, then tidying away is more important for the four-year-olds who, at primary school, will have to complete pieces of work. This may require staff to encourage finishing one activity before rushing off to begin another.

Helping children with specific needs

Arguably the most vital interventions need to be made if learning difficulties or physical difficulties are suspected. These can vary from providing a great deal of reinforcement so that the child is enabled to progress, contacting the parents and suggesting things they might do at home or asking for outside expert help. In many areas, expert help is severely limited for preschool children. Some authorities claim that they do not have the resources to support children with special needs before the age of five, so the nursery staff have to familiarise themselves (by reading the appropriate literature) about the different difficulties and try to help as best they can.

Identifying and supporting children with difficulties

Observing any group of children shows that some progress faster than others in one or more aspects of their development. This is to be expected given genetic factors, i.e. the inherited patterns of abilities, aptitudes and attitudes the children have as part of their make-up, and the environmental influences, e.g. the family practices, the cultural expectations and the exposure to experiences which have shaped the children's upbringing. Some children, however, give cause for concern, even taking the aforementioned factors into account.

This puts the nursery staff in a quandary; they have difficult decisions to make and can be unsure of what to do for the best. They may be very reluctant to alarm parents by suggesting that specialist help is required for they realise that in very young children, the maturation of the neurones (brain cells) and pathways in the brain is not yet complete. Improvement might be just around the corner; given time and support the child would be likely to catch up. But there are no guarantees that maturation will have this effect, and waiting lists for specialist help are long. If decisions to seek help are delayed, then it may not be available at all or at least not before the children go on to the next stage by which time the children and their friends are more likely to be aware of the difficulties and/or differences; this can have a negative impact on their self-esteem.

If parents can be approached in a positive way by suggesting that providing help now will benefit children's later development, i.e. that specialist input would possibly 'give them a boost', then hopefully the parents will agree to the child's name being added to a waiting list – after all, it can always be removed at any time if circumstances change. It would be ideal if these parents could meet those of a child who had benefited from the same kind of intervention to give them the reassurance they need. Due to issues of confidentiality, however, this may not be possible. Perhaps asking the specialist to explain the kind of intervention which would be appropriate would be the next best thing. Parents could then appreciate that fun activities are the new 'therapy'; indeed, that therapists, just like nursery teachers, recognise that enjoyment is the key to sustaining involvement and continual practice.

At the end of the day, the decision about whether to seek outside help rests with the parents. It is to be hoped, however, that the trust relationship which has been built up in the nursery will reassure the parents that everyone has the children's best interests at heart. At this very young age, it is unlikely that labels indicating specific learning difficulties would be attached to any child.

What can be done to help?

Some children can be described as 'slow to learn'. They function as younger children would across all aspects of their development. Often giving them an extra year in nursery provides the best solution: the context is familiar and all the basic learning skills are reinforced. Furthermore, the smaller staff:pupil ratio means that there is a little more time to plan interventions and challenges to suit the individual child, who is already well known to the staff. In a familiar context and with people they know, these children can concentrate on learning. Moreover, they will be 'the big ones' who can be helpers, thereby building their confidence.

Some parents will worry that these children will lose their friends and wonder why they have gone to 'big' school while they are still in the nursery. These tend to be parental worries: experience shows that the children will soon be immersed with new friends. The alternative, i.e. pushing them into a situation where they will not be able to cope, cannot do them any good at all and may cause long-lasting harm to their self-esteem. Different regions have differing policies about children remaining with their age group but usually the nursery can make recommendations which may or may not influence the final policy decisions.

Within what may be termed, 'global developmental delay', there can be some aspects of the child's development that are more worrying than others, especially when these impact on most learning competences. Examples are:

- poor communication skills;
- delayed or disordered language;
- limited movement control;
- poor attention and short-term memory;
- inaccurate perception;
- poor planning and organisational skills.

Some children may display only one of these aspects, but often a child will have a complex pattern of difficulties at different levels of severity. The accurate diagnosis of difficulty is made even more perplexing because the level of competence may fluctuate from day to day, due to both personal and environmental factors.

Case study: Harry

Harry's behaviour was causing severe problems. He didn't seem to be able to be still at all. When the staff tried to prevent him rushing around he became tearful and agitated, rocking back and forward or flapping his hands. Harry wasn't aggressive, but he couldn't settle to learn. The other children clearly didn't want him to play as he didn't get involved in their game. He constantly rushed off to do something else, at the same time complaining that no one would let him play. His parents were so anxious about the possibility of attention deficit hyperactivity disorder (ADHD) that a meeting with a psychologist was arranged.

Support in the nursery

As an interim measure, the psychologist had suggested some basic strategies to reduce his 'tactile insecurity'. First, Harry was given a lump of plasticine at story time so that he could mould that with his hands as he listened. He was part of a group where short stories were specially selected. He was also given a large beanbag to sit on, the explanation being that some children need extra support to compensate for poor muscle tone which causes them to flop. The staff were asked to observe Harry closely and to praise him when he did stay on his beanbag for a spell.

Interestingly and quite independently, Harry's parents decided that they should try a nutritional supplement. He had suffered from eczema as a toddler and at that time, the GP had suggested his diet should be rich in unsaturated fatty acids, e.g. fish oils, to help his dry skin which itched at night causing him to lose sleep. But as Harry would not eat fish at all, it had not been possible to follow this advice. His mum had just recently discovered capsules which act as a supplement to counteract fatty acid deficiency. Almost immediately his restlessness improved and his 'itchy skin' quietened to give him some respite. This nutritional supplement, which was not a drug, had helped their child. Other dietary advice was to examine food labels to cut out additives, e.g. giving him fresh orange juice instead of diluted squashes, butter instead of margarine and to encourage Harry to eat fish such as tuna. These were all helpful moves.

A different group of children may present with another kind of problem. They may have a discrepancy across the different aspects of their development so that one is significantly less well developed than the others. What kind of difficulties would they show?

Specific learning difficulties

Case study: Jon

Jon, aged 4 in his first session at this nursery, was very articulate. He volunteered information about happenings at home, he listened avidly at story time and could predict with some accuracy. He could even compose stories of his own and relate them to a group. The children enjoyed this and Jon became buoyed by his success as a storyteller. He could recognise numbers, count up to 20 fluently and use mathematical language appropriately.

But Jon would not try puzzles such as jigsaws or manipulative toys at all. When the staff tried to encourage him, he would approach the table as if he was going to join in and then sweep the puzzles to the floor. He would then wander off, apparently carefree and not worried that he had spoiled the other children's work. When his parents heard about this behaviour from another child he was scolded, but he told them that 'puzzles are rubbish anyway'.

Further observations revealed that Jon was avoiding the writing table. While he had managed to wield the larger, thicker paint brush, his paintings showed no form at all. They were not of the quality his oral work might have suggested. Further observations showed that he could not manipulate a pencil, using the tripod grip even when a triangular rubber support was in place.

Some strategies for support in the nursery:

- Practice in fine motor skills which will strengthen Jon's hands. Encourage him to work in the wet sand or with clay (these materials would provide resistance and so strengthen his fingers).
- Help him learn to play a simple scale or tune on the piano so that he watches each finger move. Action songs such as 'Incy, Wincy Spider' aid finger awareness and mobility.
- Check hand dominance – ask him which hand gives the best results and observe his choice of hand at the different activities to see if this is so. If he appears to be left-handed provide left-handed scissors. Have fun with singing games such as the 'Hokey Kokey' to establish his hand awareness. Make sure he is beside, not opposite, the staff so that he can copy without reversing the pattern if he is not sure.

Detailed observations of progress are essential as Jon's difficulties could be a sign of dyspraxia.

Case study: Emma

Emma completed complex puzzles with no difficulty and was keen to listen to stories. She was anxious to write and did this with control, but she rarely spoke to the other children. The staff found it hard to understand what little speech she had volunteered and consultation with Emma's parents revealed that they were concerned too. They had been hoping that time spent with children of her own age would encourage her to talk and were waiting to find out if this would be effective.

Emma's parents confirmed the staff's observations that Emma was able to understand everything that was said. She had made babbling sounds when she was a baby, and now she could follow instructions and enjoyed stories, so everyone was at a loss to know why she didn't speak clearly or confidently. Her parents were anxious that speech therapy should be requested without delay.

In the nursery, all the staff and students were asked to make sure they gave Emma time to speak – they were advised to be very calm and not to rush in to follow her non-verbal indicators or to provide answers for her. Emma's favourite story was *The Little Red Hen* so the staff read that with her every day, encouraging her to say the punchline 'So I will' and giving her lots of praise when she tried.

Through taping Emma's speech, the speech and language therapists recognised that Emma's consonants and vowels were confused and they provided her with games in which she had to practise individual letters of the alphabet (one each week), sounding them out carefully and thinking about how they sounded and where they were made, i.e. in the back or the front of her mouth. After several months of speech therapy, home practice and learning about sounds in the nursery, Emma had the confidence to tell her special helper in the nursery, 'I go to games with a talking lady – Mummy goes too'. Her speech gradually became clearer so that by the time of going into Primary 1 her teacher and classmates were able to understand her. She still didn't offer to talk much but as several of the children were quiet, her difficulty was not apparent to the other children. Gradually her confidence grew and she volunteered to talk a little more. Her parents were convinced that early speech therapy had made a huge difference.

In 2001, there were 80% more children presenting with special needs (Keen 2001). This is startling, extremely worrying and raises many questions such as are there truly many more children with difficulties and if so why?

Possible answers:

- Today's children have a very different lifestyle to those of even 20 years ago. Many have less freedom to play freely out of doors so they have less practice in the rough and tumble which promotes balance and coordination.
- Much of the environment is built up. There are fewer easily accessible open spaces for games to be played and ploys to be made up. The colourful swing parks which do exist may provide rockets as well as swings and this is good, but much of the apparatus is limiting in promoting imaginative play.
- More processed food with additives that may influence the behaviour of some children is a regular part of many diets.
- The hectic lifestyle many families choose (or have) to lead means that mealtimes together are rare. Thus time for talking together is reduced and using a knife and fork can be jettisoned when pizzas only need fingers! Opportunities for conversation – especially when the television is on – and fine motor skill development are reduced.
- Both teachers and parents are more aware of the indicators of difficulties. While this is a good thing, there is the danger that they may press the panic button too soon by making diagnostic assessments without allowing enough time for maturation. On the other hand, delaying and being cautious have their own drawbacks in that assessments may be harder to obtain. Teachers are very aware of the danger of being blamed – even sued – for not taking immediate action and may do so in order to cover themselves. They are also anxious that the child should have expert help and individual attention for more time than is possible in a primary class with 30 or more other children.
- Perhaps today, in this era of target-setting and competition, some teachers and parents are even more anxious to have the perfect child. This may cause them to compare 'the child they have' to some hypothetical notion of perfection and so discover difficulties which would not have previously worried them.

Case study: an infant teacher's experience

Kate, an experienced infant teacher, tells of her experiences and asks for guidance. She explained:

> I thought all the children in my class were getting on fine, I really did, until I went on these courses on special needs. Now I realise that there is a whole group of them showing different aspects of difficulties. What should I do? How do I know whether the children have a real problem or whether they will grow out of their difficulties? I can see where children have a problem, but is it severe enough to warrant trying to get extra help?

She went on to ask:

> If I ask for outside help for these children beyond the support we can provide in school they get a label. The difficulty is that they are then seen to be different. Is that doing them any favours?

Labelling

'Having a label' has its pros and cons. On the positive side is the fact that adults should immediately understand the child's difficulties and put strategies in place to help. The downside is that when adults are told that a child has dyspraxia or dyslexia – or any of the other special needs – the child tends to be seen as having all the difficulties of that condition. Two important factors should be borne in mind: first, that each child will have an individual pattern of difficulties which may not 'fit' any label; second, that 'the label need not stick' (Caan 1999).

It is very unlikely that children will be given labels at nursery; as maturation is ongoing some of the difficulties will be reduced if not resolved. The nursery profile which contains indicators of difficulties, however, is the first step along that road, which is why it must be comprehensive as well as accurate.

The nursery profile

The dilemma now is to decide on how much detail the recipients need. Any competence can be broken down into a myriad of tiny contributing factors, but the workload of recording them all has to be weighed against the usefulness of the information. The temptation to record 'everything' has to be avoided unless in special circumstances – a plethora of detail can be confusing or perhaps too complex to read at all!

A useful and realistic profile

One strategy is to ask, 'Can the child do it?' and if the answer is 'yes' report the name of the activity. However, if the answer is 'no' then further analysis into the underlying abilities is required. A profile always needs space for comments to allow for elaboration, e.g. that the child's progress has been disrupted for some reason or that attendance is poor.

7　Transitions

The word 'transition' usually conjures up the idea of moving from nursery to 'big' school, but the transition into nursery must be planned as well. Many, even most, children will come straight from home to nursery (see Ch. 1, 'Settling in'), but others may have attended a crèche, a private nursery or been looked after by a childminder at home. Regardless of their earlier experiences, all of the children face some degree of change and disruption to their lives. Some will look forward to the change, others will be much less confident, while a small group will find it particularly stressful. Although transition might appear to be easy for those children who have already attended a private nursery with a similar routine, they still have to meet new people in different surroundings and adapt to a new routine. And if there has been a long holiday, much of the earlier experience may be forgotten. This is why no child should be expected to stay for a whole session on the first day.

Children with a whole range of special support needs, e.g. family bereavement or breakdown, difficult behaviour, Down's syndrome and other conditions which may indicate learning difficulties, may come to nursery from a child and family centre, or they may come from home to nursery with documentation to show that they are already having physiotherapy, speech therapy or psychological help. Extra support for all of the different needs has to be planned well in advance to make sure that all these children are given the best possible start.

The new policies on inclusion mean that more children with more profound difficulties than ever before will be going into mainstream classes. The nursery, with its higher staff:pupil ratio, is a wonderful start. Sometimes, however, staff are expected to cope without prior warning!

Inter-agency meetings

It is critically important that these meetings are arranged early enough for any special resources to be in place. Health, social work and education have to get together early to ease the pathway for children who have special needs. Budgets for special needs auxiliary help are worked out well in advance of the school year, so communication from the school and health professionals has to be forthcoming in time to ensure that the appropriate help can be obtained.

Even more notice is required if the nursery has to be physically altered so that access to all parts is possible. The entrance, the toilet block and the outdoor area must allow a wheelchair to be manoeuvred with other small children present. Ramps may have to be built and a special toilet with special hand grips and possibly an alarm put in place. In the garden, a raised bed could allow a wheelchair-bound child to participate. All of these essential features take time to organise, especially if the nursery building is old making modifications difficult.

Who should attend?

Obviously, the different special needs require different groups of people to share their expertise and their special knowledge of the particular child coming to nursery. The most appropriate selection from the following list will be required:

- Parents/carers
- The key worker from the child and family centre
- A teacher from the new nursery
- The social worker
- The health visitor
- The community medical officer
- A specialist nurse, e.g. for cystic fibrosis
- A speech therapist
- A physiotherapist
- An occupational therapist
- A psychologist.

Supported transitions

A supported transition may be required. Ideally, several short visits to the nursery are made by the child accompanied by the parents and key worker in the term before the child starts. This ensures that the nursery can be adapted in the most appropriate way and gives the nursery staff time to understand the child's condition fully and the implications for learning and socialising in the nursery setting. These advance meetings also allow time for nursery staff to find out about cerebral palsy or autism or whatever the child's difficulty might be. They also allow the different groups of professionals to build the kind of relationship which will facilitate requests for immediate advice in times of crisis. Sharing queries about procedures and suggesting alternatives can happen informally and quickly when the people involved have met, understood each context and appreciated the job each has to do. There are many different groups of experts with their own kinds of knowledge – it is essential that the child benefits from them all.

Respite care

Sometimes the families of children who need support are offered respite care. The child can then be well looked after 'on holiday' to give the family a little time to recoup their resources or spend more time with their other children. Ideally, carers from these settings can attend the meetings as well in order to provide total, wrap-around care.

Transition to 'big school'

After the Easter holidays, the nursery children become interested and usually excited at the prospect of 'big school' and much can be done to smooth the way. In the nursery, a school corner can be set up allowing role play as teacher or pupil and 'Starting School' books can be used at story time. Visits to the first class can be arranged followed by discussions with the children about their experiences. Expectations and fears can be shared in an informal way.

Nursery classes within a school

This arrangement allows many transition opportunities, e.g. the nursery children taking a message to the school office and so getting to know the support staff and possibly meet the management staff; the nursery children using the school hall for movement sessions, attending the school concert or even joining in short assemblies. Sometimes older children can make reciprocal visits and arrange to see the children at play time (a buddy system). All these possibilities depend on the proximity of the nursery to the particular venues, but whenever possible they should be arranged to familiarise the children with their next school environment.

The children can make short visits to their new classroom and, perhaps most important of all, they can be introduced to the huge open space and the mass of moving strangers that constitute break time.

Case study: one nursery's strategies to aid transition

Laura, a nursery nurse, explains:

> Our nursery is adjacent to the school playground. It's a large, inner-city school and the children enjoy letting off steam. The playground auxiliaries are kept busy sorting out squabbles and there's always lots of noise. We planned to introduce our children to this so that they wouldn't be alarmed when they had to survive alone.
>
> First of all we thought through what new things the children would have to be able to do. We decided these were:
>
> 1. to make up games that did not need the toys or big apparatus which they were used to in the nursery;
> 2. to understand the playground rules, e.g. that they were not allowed to go out the gates even if adults left them open;
> 3. to know that playground auxiliaries were there to help them, even though they did not teach them in the classroom.
>
> The nursery nurses then took six children at a time into the infant playground. At first the children stayed close, but after a few infant children invited them to play some of them went off quite happily, while the more timid ones began to make up a chasing game of their own. They explained that they were glad that playing with balls was kept to the grass area. The auxiliaries came over to meet the children on the first few occasions and that broke the ice.
>
> Back in the nursery they introduced some 'toy-free' play times 'just like the big school' and left the children to see what they would do. Some copied the older children, playing 'Follow my leader' games and chasing round more than they had ever done before, while other children played the circle games that they had enjoyed in the nursery so we felt that opportunities to prepare the children had been very worthwhile.

Passing on information to the infant school

The infant class may well be taking in children from several nurseries so passing on a photo of each child along with a nursery profile helps the teacher greet each child by name on their first day (he or she may have 25–30 children whom he or she has only met once or twice).

Some regions provide transition documents while others allow nurseries to create their own; this should be checked.

Passing on information to the parents

A transition leaflet can be offered to the parents (and posted on the parents' notice board, see below) so that they may make reference to it just as they did with the parents' booklet issued at the start of the nursery year. They will receive details from the school so there is no need to duplicate this information; however, some advice about preparation is often welcomed.

Transition: Informal Information Exchange Document

From Nursery to Key Stage 1/Primary 1

Child's Name: .... Date of Birth: ....

Male ☐   Female ☐   EAL: Yes ☐   No ☐

	Excellent	Good	Needs support	Comment
Behaviour				
Self-confidence				
Fine motor skills				
Gross motor skills				
Speech – articulation/clarity				
Vocabulary				
Listening skills				
Counting skills				
Creative and expressive skills				
Attention/concentration				

Health: Please comment re attendance and any advice

Does the child attend a: Does the child:

Speech therapist	
Occupational therapist	
Psychologist	

Wear glasses	
Use an inhaler	
Have any allergies (if yes please say which)	

Comments:

Figure 7.1 A simple, sample transition document (for schools)

Transition Leaflet

When [child's name] goes on to the infant school they will be expected to be more independent. It is important to remember this when buying clothes/school uniform and equipment for them.

It can be helpful for them to have:

- Shoes with velcro fasteners; avoid laces! The children will have to change their shoes for PE or other activities in the hall and no teacher has time to tie 25 pairs of laces. Some schools require the children to wear indoor shoes. Remember to check their size as the children's feet grow. Pull-on ones with elastic, slip-on sandals or again velcro fasteners are ideal.
- Clothes which are easy to put on and take off. Avoid clothes with tight armholes or waistbands because the children will have difficulty getting them off and on again at PE and they usually hate to be last.
- Name every item of clothing and equipment such as pencil cases, bus pass holders etc., i.e. everything you hope to have home again. Remove any sibling name tabs – a new teacher may not realise that a garment originally belonged to an older brother or sister and be confused by not recognising the name! Remember to name shorts for PE as these are often forgotten.
- Lunchboxes and juice beakers. While these have to be secure so that the contents don't spill, small hands have to be able to open them. It is a good idea to test this before purchasing the containers and to let the child practise at home. Some pre-wrapped foods can be difficult to open too, e.g. some yoghurt lids need a strong pull; the contents can spill and distress the child, quite apart from spoiling clothes. It is best to decant the yoghurt into a small plastic jar. If the child cannot cope then parents should notify the teacher who will pass the message to a lunch auxiliary to ensure the child has the intended meal.
- Pencil cases. The children do not need dozens of pencils or felt pens. Very often these are provided in the infant classes so if the children feel a pencil case is important, then limit the number of items inside. Then there are fewer to be lost!
- Toys at school. Parents will appreciate that although children enjoy bringing a favourite toy to school, keeping track of them all is quite a job. Unless the children are distressed, it is best to keep the toys at home. Perhaps the toy could accompany the child to school and then go home with Mum or Dad? Parents can explain to the child that while they are busy working, the toy might be lonely or even mislaid.

Bridging the gap

Many infant classes now follow the nursery's lead and provide some time and resources for the children to learn through play. However, because the child:adult ratio is increased, the main teaching mode is in groups rather than on an individual basis which may make it more formal. This apart, all the preparation that has gone on in the nursery, i.e. all the creative work, the role play, the opportunities for movement, problem solving and all the other kinds of intellectual and social stimulation provides the kind of foundation which should help every child make the most of their time in school. We hope they do!

Catalogues

Early years resource catalogues

Community Playthings
Brightling Road
Robertsbridge
East Sussex TN32 5DR
Tel: 01580 883301
Website: www.communityproducts.com
Wooden toys, climbing equipment, furniture, storage, large blocks

Insect Lore
PO Box 1420
Kiln Farm
Milton Keynes MK19 6ZH
Tel: 01908 563338
Website: www.insectlore.co.uk
Science and nature

Learning and Teaching Scotland
74 Victoria Crescent Road
Glasgow G12 9JN
Tel: 08700 100297
Email: orders@LstScotland.com
Website: www.ltscotland.com
IT software

Mantra – Dual Language
5 Alexandra Grove
London N12 8NU
Tel: 020 8445 5123
Email: info@mantrapublishing.com
Website: www.mantrapublishing.com
Books, posters, teachers' resources

REM
Great Western House
Langport
Somerset TA10 9YU
Tel: 01458 254700
Email: sales@r-e-m.co.uk
Preschool and primary software, digital content

Rompa
Goyt Side Road
Chesterfield
Derby S40 2PH
Tel: 0800 056 2323
Email: Sales@rompa.com
Spinning top

General catalogues

Gault Education
Hyde Buildings
Johnson Brook Road
Hyde
Cheshire SK14 4QT
Tel: 0845 120 3005
Website: www.gault-educational.co.uk

Hope Education
Hyde Buildings
Ashton Road
Hyde
Cheshire SK14 4SH
Tel: 0845 120 2055
Website: www.hope-education.co.uk

Books for preschool children

The following is just a small selection of all the wonderful books available for the nursery.

Janet and Allan Ahlberg, *Each Peach, Pear, Plum* (Puffin)

Jez Alborough, *Bare Bear* (Hodder & Stoughton)

Althea, *Smith the Lonely Hedgehog*

Giles Andreae and David Wojtowycz, *Rumble in the Jungle* (Orchard Picture Books)

Ian Black and Sarah Williams, *Round and Round the Garden: Play Rhymes for Young Children* (Oxford University Press)

Ruth Brown, *A Dark, Dark Tale* (Mantra Dual Language)

Lisa Bruce and Stephen Waterhouse, *Engines, Engines: An Indian Counting Rhyme* (Bloomsbury Paperbacks)

Eric Carle, *The Very Hungry Caterpillar* (Mantra Dual Language)

Faustin Charles and Michael Terry, *The Selfish Crocodile* (Bloomsbury Paperbacks)

Helen Cooper, *The Bear Under the Stairs* (Picture Corgi)

Helen Cooper, *Pumpkin Soup* (Corgi)

Penny Dale, *Ten in the Bed* (Walker Books)

Alan Durant, *Snake Supper* (Picture Lions)

John Foster, *Another Very First Poetry Book* (Oxford University Press)

Mike Gibbie and Barbara Nascimberi, *Small Bad Dog's Remembering Day* (Macmillan)

Sarah Hayes and Barbara Firth, *The Grumpalump* (Walker Books)

Sarah Hayes and Toni Goffe, *Clap Your Hands: Action Rhymes* (Walker Books)

Sarah Hayes and Toni Goffe, *Stamp Your Feet: Action Rhymes* (Walker Books)

Diana Henry, *The Very Noisy Night* (Little Tiger Press)

Pat Hutchins, *Don't Forget the Bacon!* (Bodley Head)

Jack Kent, *There's No Such Thing as a Dragon* (Blackie)

Alan MacDonald (illustrated by Gwyneth Williamson), *Beware of the Bears!* (Magi)

Christine Macintyre (music by Mike Carter), *Jingle Time – Jingles and Music with Teacher's Notes for Early Years Children* (David Fulton Publishers)

Bill Martin and Eric Carle, *Brown Bear, Brown Bear, What Do You See?* (Picture Lions)

Bill Martin and Eric Carle, *Polar Bear, Polar Bear, What Do You Hear?* (Puffin)

Terry Mittan and Ant Parker, *Terrific Trains* (Kingfisher)

Inga Moore, *Six Dinner Sid* (Macdonald Young Books)

Nick Sharrat, *Don't Put Your Finger in the Jelly, Nelly* (Scholastic Press)

Elfrida Vipont and Raymond Briggs, *The Elephant and the Bad Baby* (Puffin)

Martin Waddell, *Owl Babies* (Walker Books)

Steve Weatherill, *Goodnight Goz* (Frances Lincoln)

Colin West, *'I Don't Care' Said the Bear* (Walker Giggle Club)

Zoeltall, *It's Pumpkin Time!* (Scholastic)

Bibliography

Bee, H. (2000) *The Developing Child* (9th edn). London: Allyn & Bacon.

Bennett, N., Wood, L. and Rogers, S. (1999) *Teaching through Play: Teacher's Thinking and Classroom Practice*. Buckingham: Open University Press.

Caan, W. (1999) 'Foreword' in Portwood, M., *Developmental Dyspraxia: A Manual for Parents and Professionals* (2nd edn). London: David Fulton Publishers.

Cohen, D. (1997) *The Development of Play*. New York: New York University Press.

Department for Education and Employment (DfEE) (2000) *Curriculum Guidance for the Foundation Stage*. London: DfEE.

Deponio, P. and Macintyre, C. (2003) *Supporting Children with Specific Learning Difficulties: Looking beyond the Label to Assess the Whole Child*. London: Routledge.

HMI (1997) *A Curriculum Framework for Children in their Pre-school Year*. Edinburgh: Scottish Office.

Keen, D. (2001) *Specific Neurodevelopmental Disorders*. Paper presented at the Conference on the Needs of Children with Specific Developmental Difficulties, Bishop Auckland, February 2001.

Macintyre, C. (2001a) *Enhancing Learning through Play*. London: David Fulton Publishers.

Macintyre, C. (2001b) *Dyspraxia 5–11*. London: David Fulton Publishers.

Macintyre, C. (2002) *Play for Children with Special Educational Needs*. London: David Fulton Publishers.

Macintyre, C. (2002b) *Jingle Time: Rhymes and songs for Early Years Learning*. London: David Fulton Publishers.

Piaget, J. (1964) *The Psychology of the Child*. New York: Basic Books.